The Dramatic Method of Teaching

Harriet Finlay-Johnson

THE "TIG" SHED IN COURSE OF CONSTRUCTION

THE DRAMATIC METHOD
OF TEACHING

BY

HARRIET FINLAY–JOHNSON

EDITED BY

ELLEN M. CYR

AUTHOR OF THE CHILDREN'S READERS

GINN AND COMPANY

BOSTON · NEW YORK · CHICAGO · LONDON

187518

The Athenæum Press

GINN AND COMPANY · PRO-
PRIETORS · BOSTON · U.S.A.

PREFACE

I undertook with great pleasure the task of editing this book for the inspiration and guidance of the teachers in America. Every page is imbued with the spirit of joy and life, — natural, spontaneous life, — recognizing the rights of a child to his own point of view with his own limitations.

Education *is* life, not just the preparation *for* life. Some one has said that education is "being at home in God's world," and another educator gives the following beatitude: "Blessed are they who do hunger and thirst after the knowledge of how to direct instead of suppress the spontaneous activities of childhood, seeking to transmute what is evil into good, for they shall make happy and competent and well-behaved children."

The best teachers are those who lead their pupils into activities which, based upon the fundamental instincts of child nature, are to test and examine everything and to attempt all feats.

Miss Finlay-Johnson recognizes her pupils as little men and women who have a right to appropriate just that part of this world which belongs to childhood, and in her school the children live in a world of their own and look upon life through their own childish vision. They enact again the events of history, literature, and geography, and fill even the arithmetic lessons with life and action. In the study of history the characters are released from their imprisonment between the covers of the books ; they don their regalia and, stepping out of the prosy pages, live their lives again and perform once more their deeds of courage and prowess. This dramatic work brings the children into closer relationship, awakening sympathy between the pupils and teacher, and fosters class spirit. It also gives the forward children opportunities for leadership, and offers a natural outlet for spontaneity and enthusiasm. Ingenuity, individuality, and imagination are developed when the children make their own stage properties, as they were led to do by Miss Finlay-Johnson.

A child enters school during the years of the play period. " Shades of the prison house begin to close upon the growing boy," and it seems hardly fair to confine him in a schoolroom during this time. Activities at this age mean much more than objects to the child, and, in justice to his development, every means to educate him by play should be employed. If he finds himself repressed on every side, he becomes discouraged and loses interest in his lessons ; and the depression which is likely to follow retards his mental growth. His interest is most quickly aroused in results brought about by his own activities. Wise is the teacher who fosters the enthusiasm and elasticity of these early years, and helps the child to realize the forces that exist within him.

This dramatic work should be kept simple. Miss Finlay-Johnson realizes this and also the danger of working for theatrical effects. She avoids this danger by engaging the whole class in most of the plays, and by letting the children suggest their own methods of acting. It is interesting to note the way in which Miss Finlay-Johnson introduces acting into the various branches of study. The dolls in the geography lessons impersonate the inhabitants of the various countries, and the children interest themselves in the clothing adapted to the various countries and climates. A prominent educator says, "there is more philosophy and poetry in a single doll than in a thousand books."

I hope many of our American teachers will learn lessons from the experiences of Miss Finlay-Johnson in her work in "the little school on the Sussex Downs, where children and teachers lived for a space in the world of romance and happiness." She preaches "the gospel of happiness in childhood for those who will be the world's workers and fighters to-morrow," and it is her conviction that "fleeting childhood's days should be filled with joy."

Acknowledgment is made for permission to use illustrations from the dramatic work in the schools of New Haven, Connecticut, and Holyoke, Massachusetts.

ELLEN M. CYR

CONTENTS

FULL-PAGE ILLUSTRATIONS

xi

THE DRAMATIC METHOD
OF TEACHING

THE DRAMATIC METHOD
OF TEACHING

CHAPTER I

INTRODUCTION

IN my endeavor to write a practical account of the way I taught my school children by the *dramatic method*, I think it will be useful to preface the more practical chapters with a few introductory words. I feel sure that all educationists worthy of the name will agree that at the present day, more than ever before, only the very best will be good enough for the education of our children. Yet I cannot help thinking also that, in our conscientious search for that best, we (even the most thoughtful of us) may lose sight of the *child* in our hunt for the *method*. It was my endeavor to treat with children rather than with methods and theories which led me to throw more and more of the initial effort on to the children themselves. The school in which my experiments were carried out was an English village school of about eighty-five older pupils and forty-five primary children — the latter with my sister in charge. There, twelve years ago, I found myself in the position of head teacher; and it was then

3

that I came to the conclusion that there was a great need of a radical change. So little was there of initiative or originality on the part of the children themselves, that I felt sure nothing short of a surgical operation — a complete cutting away of old habits and the formation of a new school tradition — would meet the case. The first aid which I invoked was "nature study," mainly from its æsthetic standpoint ; and from the very first I realized that, to be of any value, it must be nature *really studied by the child himself.* It must not be nature filtered through pictorial illustration, textbook, dried specimen, and scientific terms, finally dribbled into passive children's minds minus the joy of assimilation ; but it must be the real study of living and working nature, absorbed in the open air under conditions which allow for free movement under natural discipline. And since nature is the storehouse from which poet and artist draw their inspiration, it naturally follows that we found it but a short step from the study of the open book of nature into the Elysian fields of literature and the arts. Nature study then became the basis of every possible lesson ; and the school nature gardens and nature rambles supplied subject matter for lessons in singing, reading, writing, arithmetic, drawing, painting, recitation, composition, grammar, and much of the geography.

It was because the lessons in history could not be so well connected with nature study, and therefore lacked the living interest which the other subjects now acquired from nature, that the historical play in my school came to be evolved. A child learns, and retains what he is learning,

"IVANHOE"—THE ARREST OF MALVOISIN

(Note the proud dignity assumed by the principals)

5

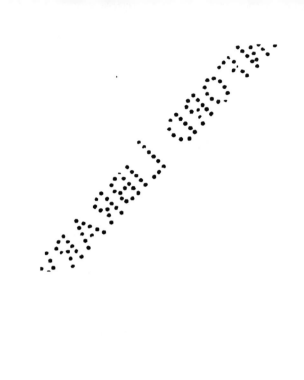

better by actually *seeing* and *doing* things, which is a guiding principle of kindergartners. There is not a very marked difference between the ages of the children who enjoy learning by kindergarten games and of the so-called " older pupils." Why not continue the principle of the kindergarten game in the school for older pupils? I did so, but with this difference : instead of letting the teacher originate or conduct the play, I demanded that, just as the individual himself must study nature and not have it studied for him, the play must be the child's own. However crude the action or dialogue from the adult's point of view, it would fitly express the stage of development arrived at by the child's mind, and would therefore be valuable *to him* as a vehicle of expression and assimilation (which is, after all, what we need), rather than a finished product pleasing to the more cultivated mind of an adult, and perhaps uninteresting to a child.

So far as originality is concerned, I believe all children are original. But the elementary-school tradition (as we have been forced to know it hitherto) has followed faithfully the lead of the first schoolmasters — who catered to pupils of mature years. This tradition tacitly presupposes the development of qualities and faculties of mind which are not developed in the child of tender years ; thus nature's plan is violated. To study a child who is attending a school conducted under such conditions will not result in our finding out much about the natural, normal child. A child in such a case will have learned to *suppress* himself — his originality — and not to *express* himself.

Language and facial expression are vehicles of thought (at least, they are in childhood). But in schools where the lessons are conducted on the lecture and question-and-answer principle, thought and language are limited and facial expression may be *nil*. The question, of necessity, determines the trend of the answer, and, to a certain extent, suggests the terms of the answer.

In order that I might see how far the beauties of nature, literature, and the arts had been comprehended and appreciated by my pupils, I realized that I must get them to converse freely with me (or at all events where I could hear their real conversations), and not merely to listen to me or answer my questions. Here was the main difficulty (and here will lie the difficulty for those teachers who desire to base their children's school lives on rational and natural lines) — to obtain free, natural, and spontaneous conversation, real self-expression from pupils who have learned as a tradition that " Talking in school is against the rules! " Here, again, nature study served me ; children once trained to observe rightly soon have no difficulty in telling about what they have seen, and lose all shyness in discussing the whys and wherefores of natural phenomena with others who have observed the same things. The four steps to original conversations and to an improved vocabulary were :

1. I first trained the children to *see* the world of nature around them.

2. I encouraged them to *tell* me what they saw.

3. I showed them where to find their earliest impressions confirmed and crystallized, which was their introduction to good literature, with its (to them) new vocabulary.

4. I led them to look for "reasons why," by means of free discussions, and to imagine for themselves the gleam, "the light that never was, on sea or land."

And all this time my pupils were developing rapidly — acquiring natural manners with a lack of self-consciousness; enlarging their vocabulary with the knowledge of how to use it; attacking difficulties with zest, and with an absence of nervousness or self-distrust; taking a cheerful, bright outlook on life with no tendency to worry. Surely such habits are a more valuable foundation for a life's career than the mere ability to spell a large number of extraordinary words, to work a certain number of sums on set rules, or to be able to read whole pages of printed matter without being able to comprehend a single idea, or to originate any new train of thought.

Having thus brought my school to a condition in which the pupils had really lost and forgotten *the relationships of teacher and pupil,* by substituting those of fellow workers, friends, and playmates, I had now to set to work to use to full advantage this condition of affairs. It was now quite possible to play any game in school without fear of the pupils getting out of hand, confused, or too boisterous. There could be plenty of liberty without license, because the teacher, being a companion to and fellow worker with the pupils, had a strong moral hold on them and shared in the citizen's right of holding an opinion, being heard, therefore, not as "absolute monarch," but on the same grounds as the children themselves. Hence every one exerted his or her individual powers to make the plays a success (which in the children's opinion meant their being real and lifelike), and it was the equal right of teacher or child to say, "So-and-so is n't playing the game," or in some other way to criticize the actions of others. It was, moreover, a point of honor that pupils so criticized should take the matter in good part and endeavor to conform to the rules of the game.

Our first plays were *historical* and were based on the historical novel, because

1. The children were already interested in reading them, and had formed fairly dramatic pictures of them in their own minds.

2. I desired that, at first, the children should act real characters rather than mythical or fairy creations. This did away with acting for display in the usual school-entertainment style, which would have detracted considerably from the educational value, in that it would have fostered self-consciousness or nervousness.

3. The pupils had already, with my coöperation, formed a school library for use during school hours, and this contained a sufficient number and variety of books out of which to extract material for the

REDCROSS KNIGHTS IN ARMOR OF TEA PAPER

dialogues and arrangements of their plays. In these books they had already found many scenes dealing with real historical personages, which were easily adapted to the needs of school games and plays.

The point which I should like particularly to emphasize is that the earliest plays should deal with *real* persons. Children are generally sincere and are most interested in a story that is true.

A great advantage of this new method of learning lessons by means of playing and acting them, lay in the fact that it was not absolutely necessary to have the lessons in one particular room ; they could as easily, or more easily, be played in the open air. Frequently we acted our history plays on the downs, in overgrown chalk pits, or just in our own school playground.

The advantage of this adaptability of situation lies in the fact that more movement and open-air conditions make for the improved health of teachers and pupils alike. In the history of education we appear to have arrived at a time when we have to consider the advisability — or the reverse — of giving our pupils what is termed a practical education. Too often, it seems, the practical degenerates into the merely technical or utilitarian, and may usurp time which should be given to the humanities. Every one agrees that childhood should be — and nearly always is — the happiest time of life ; when that is once over, there is " something lost and gone " that no subsequent happiness quite atones for. If this be true, then am I wrong when I claim that childhood should be a time for merely absorbing big stores of sunshine for possible future dark times? And what do I mean by sunshine but just the things for which nature implanted (in the best and highest part of us) an innate desire? The joy of knowing the beauties of the living world around us and of probing its mysteries; the delights of finding sympathetic thoughts in the best of English literature (a literature unrivaled in the world!); the gradual appreciation of the beautiful in art; the desire which all these bring to burning youth to be up and "doing likewise"; the awakening of the young enthusiasm, even of merely evanescent youthful dreams, instead of the soul-deadening monotony and limitation of technical instruction — these are the things that count. Let the boy who delights in experiment and investigation follow his bent, and, when he himself is ready and eager for it, then supply the necessary technical instruction. Do not damp and kill the fires of young enthusiasm; they make the world go round. Our dreamers have been our real workers after all; they "dreamed dreams and saw visions" and probed things new, while they of the earth, earthy, were content to toil mechanically, as beasts having no understanding. You cannot turn out scientist or artist without a training in the humanities. And we are not required to *teach* the humanities, but to allow our boys and girls in their natural enthusiasm to absorb them from the environment which we can, at least, help to place around them.

Curiously enough the most striking result of teaching by means of the "play" in school is that children become

really practical in the best sense of the word, although we
set out to ignore the practical and pay attention to the
humanities.

And one other plea for the dramatic method of teaching in school: it makes for greater happiness of both
pupils and teachers. We all do our best when we are
happy. Most of us are happier when conscious of giving
pleasure to others. A great many persons are of the opinion that, "as the teacher, so the class." I believe, at all
events, that the temper of the teacher must necessarily
react on the class; and I know that thunderclouds of
impatience or mists of disappointment are quickly dis-
pelled by the sight of happy, healthy children entering
with zest into their interesting dramatic plays; and that
hardened and deadened indeed must be the teacher who
can resist the happiness radiated by children anxious to
play well, and looking for the encouragement shown by
the approbation of fellow pupils and teacher.

It may be argued that all these results might possibly
be obtained in the usual school routine, by making the
ordinary lessons more interesting by means of pictorial
illustrations or by the teacher's telling the children stories
inculcating the lessons in hand. And I reply that it is
more in keeping with child nature not to sit constantly
"as a passive bucket to be pumped into." I know that,
as a child, while I promptly forgot all my "school" history (taught, no doubt, in what ought to have been the
most interesting fashion, with anecdote and illustration),
I have still a clear and lively recollection of the history

(and other things) which I acted with my chums after school hours. As a matter of fact, my pupils remember an enormous amount of detailed history and fact, not to mention such things as genealogical tables (bane of all children), dates, and statistics, which they have absorbed unconsciously during their plays and in the preparation of them.

Probably most people have recollections of the time in their life when action seemed the keynote of their character. Robert Louis Stevenson, who understood children better than most people, says: "We grown-up people can tell ourselves a story, all the while sitting quietly by the fire. This is exactly what a child cannot do, or does not do — at least, when he can do anything else. He works all with lay figures and stage properties. When his story comes to the fighting he must rise, get something by way of a sword, and have a set-to with a piece of furniture until he is out of breath."

Young pupils entering our school from another very soon fell into the ways and discipline of ours; which, I think, showed that our method worked on natural lines, although it was a contrast to that generally prevailing.

I remember being much struck by hearing the inspector of our district say at an educational meeting that very few women teachers possessed a sense of humor — or at least he never found them exercising it. I have found it a great safety valve. How often a sense of humor at the right moment may prevent the tragedy of life from striking too deep! By humor I do not mean the silly frivolity

which characterizes so many children, — the giggling at
mere foolishness, which would, of course, upset any school,
— but just the ability to see the humorous side when it
ought to be seen. We frequently had amusing little unre-
hearsed effects in our plays which might have resulted in
quarrels or teasing, and so upset " plays " in school. Then
it was that the ability to " see the joke " saved the situation.
I think a sense of humor — duly harnessed — is a valuable
asset even for a business man (although I did not profess
to be training business men — Heaven forbid !). On one
occasion we were acting the insurrection of Jack Cade, and
Cade was being slain in Iden's garden. He should have
said : " Oh, I am slain ! Famine and no' other hath slain
me." What he did say was : " Oh, I am slain ! Salmon
and no other hath slain me." A hearty laugh interrupted
his beautiful death peroration. When we explained his slip
no one laughed more heartily than he. But it was remark-
able that once the laugh was legitimately and naturally out,
every one fell to once more with the play.

CHAPTER II

THE TEACHING OF HISTORY BY PLAYS

OUR first attempt at drama as a legitimate school lesson was concerned with history. We had been reading Sir Walter Scott's " Ivanhoe " as an adjunct to the study of the reign of Richard Cœur de Lion and his times. I think we were all thoroughly imbued with the atmosphere of romance and *derring-do*, and the boys in particular seemed ready for suiting the action to the word. The fire was laid; it needed but the match to start it! And here it should be noticed that the foundation and basis of our play was literature — not from the ordinarily accepted school " reader " containing a little bit about cotton, a little bit about coal, a scrappy extract from a " good " writer, with a poem about an impossible little girl who sewed " as long as her eyes could see " (so bad for her eyes, too!); the whole interlarded with moral maxims, conveying practically nothing to a child, and seasoned with a pinch of " tables " and another of " difficult " words in columns! No. In our school the whole book as it left the mind of its writer is placed on the open library shelf to be read by every interested pupil.

The practical-minded person will probably now be interested to have a description of our first play. It was a rainy day. Long play out of doors had been impossible ; so I started with a good supply of bottled energy and "instinct for play" ready to command. A little talk with the children of the upper classes and a discussion on the characters in "Ivanhoe" led to such remarks from the boys as, "If *I* had been So-and-so, I should have done so-and-so"; and as play out of doors was out of the question, some one soon suggested, "Could n't we play at 'Ivanhoe' indoors?" From that time I had no further doubts as to whether the play in school could be successfully managed. But to outsiders there was nothing brilliant in our first attempt.

To us who were " in it," the schoolroom was really the lists at Ashby de la Zouch, or any other place our imagination desired, but an outsider could see only the restricted space in front of an ordinary class. No time was wasted at first in arranging scenes or casting parts. It took but a few seconds for the boys to settle on a rosy, rotund boy for a jovial Friar Tuck, who at once deposited himself under a high, spindle-legged desk which he dubbed his hermit's cell. " I 'm the Black Knight," said another, dragging his black jersey over his head for a suit of chain mail. " Let me be your horse," volunteered another, proffering the necessary "back." Soon the play was in full swing, although it might not have seemed encouraging to the enthusiast (burning to "improve" the children) to hear Friar Tuck, forgetting the text of the book, retort "Shan't," when the Black Knight thundered with his heavy "pointer" on the spindle-legged desk, demanding admittance or "the road." The same Friar Tuck, when told by his onlookers that he ought to sing loudly, improvised quite an appropriate refrain to the words "Tol-de-rol-lol." No one laughed, and none were at all irreverent, when he changed the tune to, "While shepherds watched their flocks by night," as the nearest substitute he could find for a monkish Latin chant. There was plenty of interest, plenty of life, no ill-temper, and a sufficiency of self-expression both verbal and facial.

It has always been an axiom in matters of school method that one of the first essentials in teaching any subject should be, "First arouse the *desire to know*." When our pupils began to dramatize their lessons, they at once developed a keen desire to know many things which hitherto had been matters of pure indifference to them. For instance, after their initial performance of scenes from "Ivanhoe," they soon began to study the book closely to supply deficiencies in dialogue; and when dialogue was rendered according to the book, it had to be memorized (voluntarily), and this led to searching questions after meanings and allusions, some of which the older pupils soon learned to find in the dictionary. Here, then, was "English" studied voluntarily by young country children, to the enrichment of their vocabulary and the satisfactory rendering of plays for their own recreation. An enormous amount of general knowledge can be acquired in the hunt for meanings and derivations of words. For example, the sentences: "Doth the Grand Master allow me this combat?" "I may not deny what thou hast challenged, if the maid accepts thee as her champion," led to questions from the young actor impersonating the Grand Master as to what he was Grand Master of, and a consequent description of the order of Knights Templars, Crusaders, and the Holy Wars. This further led up to an allusion to the fact that a preceptory of the Knights Templars once existed not far from the school, and so to some local Church history. By the time the subject was exhausted every one had a good knowledge of it acquired pleasantly and permanently. They had made acquaintance with such terms as "palmers," "minstrels," "tournament," "chivalry," and "challenge"; and they had learned something about the way in which trade had extended and improved through the spirit of adventure which prompted men to travel and extend their horizon and experience.

Each subsequent performance of scenes from "Ivanhoe" showed a marvelous improvement in knowledge and intelligence of the right kind. The pupils themselves, even while inventing probable conversations not recorded verbatim in the book, either consciously or unconsciously kept up the style and "period" in their own diction. They showed the greatest resourcefulness in getting over difficulties such as must occur when boys and girls have to leave school permanently or be absent temporarily. Always one or another would come forward ready and anxious to do the necessary work. The pupils themselves suggested costume and stage properties, which the girls contrived out of silver-paper tea wrappings supplied from their homes. What mattered it if the mystic words " Ceylon Tea, $0.30

per pound" appeared writ large in sable on the hero's shield? *We* saw only the shield of a Red Cross Knight. Such delightful surprises, too, would the boys spring on us! One morning it was a set of horse brasses bestowed on the joyful recipient by a teamster. Picture how delighted the crowd was in the playground that morning when the proud owner produced them and fitted them on the "war horse"; how, of course, Ivanhoe, the champion, must have that horse; how the eager crowd trooped in to show their treasures to me; and how truly good and happy they were when, disregarding the regular schedule, we rehearsed, and I raised no objection to the war horse's curvetting, stamping, and jingling its brasses. Why, it was a *real* tournament!

Then, of course, the question arose as to what would be the proper song for Friar Tuck to sing if he might not sing "While shepherds watched," which ended in a pupil's discovering a song which *he* thought appropriate and which turned out to be "There were three ravens sat on a tree— Hey-adown-hey derry derry down," which was, I think, a sufficient advance on the first attempt to prove encouraging to the most pessimistic of pedagogues. On an inquiry being raised for a tune for "Troll the brown bowl to me, bully boy," none was forthcoming, so Friar Tuck improvised quite in the style of the "Three Ravens." But eyes, ears, and minds were kept alert, and, joy of joys, one day an inspector visited the school who, when the song time arrived, could supply the tune. He sang it over once to the most attentive audience I have ever known, and when

Photograph by Clarke and Hyde

THE CORONATION OF WILLIAM AND MARY

(Court ladies in thin "priceless" window curtains. Note the scepter and sword of state)

23

he had gone away every child knew that tune and could sing lustily, "Ho, jolly Jenkin — I spy a knave drinking." I contrasted this with some of the laborious lessons on school songs that I have known — dead bones of songs, having no responsive chords in the hearts of boys and girls!

I feel convinced that my pupils, while playing, had learned far more of the English language, history, and withal romance, than I could ever have *taught* them by means of blackboard, columns of classified words, and Latin " roots " more suited to adult students possessed of a goodly store of voluntary attention and will power — to whom, by the way, I do not believe it would be very enthralling! And surely there is no such virtue in blackboard and chalk that they should be deemed essential in the teaching of all subjects in school. How much more in keeping with child nature is it to conceal the " powder" in the " jam," and to work with live puppets at play so that the end is reached through pleasant means.

Our first plays were what I term *adapted* plays worked up from historical novels ; and when I had watched and helped through the first trial play, I began to see how it might be possible to throw more of the actual lessons, including their preparation and arrangement, on to the pupils themselves. I had long felt instinctively that the ordinary " notes of lessons "— even the best of them — were open to serious objection. For the best of notes, prepared by the teacher with laborious care overnight, presuppose an attitude of mind which may, in the morning, be missing from the class as a whole or from individual children. The teacher who prepares her notes and says, " Now I will say this and the pupils will reply so-and-so," finds that her "best laid schemes" may "gang a-gley," and that the unexpected most often happens, for the pupils' minds may not work according to the prepared "notes," and friction is the result instead of harmony. Besides, more than half the benefit of the lesson lies, in my opinion, in the act of preparing it, in hunting its materials out of hidden sources and bringing them into shape. Most people know that the best way to learn a thing is to try to impart it. If any weakness in knowledge exists, it appears directly we try to impart our facts consecutively. How much better, for instance, it is to hunt out one's own botanical specimens and study them in their own native haunts than to have a set of dried specimens, carefully collected and preserved by some one else, put into one's hands, together with a full explanation and description of their peculiarities, order, class, and habitat!

If the pupils know that they have to prepare certain scenes in order that they may, by such agency, impart certain facts to their fellow students, they immediately feel the responsibility and derive the full benefit from the lesson because they "find it" themselves, little by little, and are receptive in the highest degree because they intend at once making use of what they have found. They learn to "feel their feet" under them, — to stand alone, — to find and use their own powers.

Children have a wonderful faculty for teaching other children and learning from them. Uncontrolled, this faculty is generally used for getting one another into mischief, but diverted into other channels it may have a great influence for good. Children know by instinct how to get ideas into their companions' minds where a teacher will fail for lack of the sympathetic touch. Another strong argument in favor of allowing children to impart knowledge to others is that the pupils in any one class will almost always be from the same neighborhood, and limited to the same vocabulary; hence they will find the correct terms of expression to convey the necessary intelligence to their hearers. I have frequently found this occurring in our improvised school plays, and have been delighted to hear clever paraphrases and translations into everyday language, showing, as they did, such complete grasp of the author's meaning.

It was not only boys who could adapt plays. Suitable parts and plays were found for and by the girls. In " Ivanhoe," of course there was a Rebecca and a Rowena ; and nothing could have excelled the simplicity and quiet dignity with which they prepared and went through their parts. Naturally in historical plays boys' parts predominated, but the girls did their full share of assisting in the preparation for them and in making notes of all the scenes which had to be compiled or invented. This brings me to an important point in the dramatization of lessons. The clerical side is by no means neglected; it is, in fact, extremely arduous, but the children are unconscious of this, since the work is voluntary and determined in amount by themselves. Having found by disappointing experience that " lovely " speeches, drawn from, perhaps, two or three different books, were forgotten at the critical moment or rendered badly, the pupils made a point of writing out their speeches in full and *in their own time!* Their reward was that they convinced their audiences.

One can easily see how children may unconsciously absorb the art of spelling by encountering new words during the act of writing out notes or parts. And similarly they fall into the art of good composition and style in just the way that we grown-ups model and remodel our style — on the plan of unconsciously imitating that of good writers with a dash of ourselves thrown in. Here, then, are two of the " three R " bogies tackled without tears — *reading* and *'riting:* reading for information and immediate profit (not to speak of longer deferred and more lasting results, of which more anon), which is "reading with intelligence," and this no one can deny; and writing, not a mere "exercise" for the sake of writing and correction, with visions of the waste-paper basket looming large in the background, but writing for a purpose and for preservation for present and future use.

The *sources* from which the pupils drew their adapted plays were always placed within their reach. In one corner of the schoolroom the boys themselves have erected four long shelves, made out of disused desks. On these shelves we formed a collection of books, including as many good historical novels as we could, and endeavoring to obtain at least one good novel on each reign or period of English history. Such books as Lytton's " Harold " and "The Last of the Barons," Kingsley's " Heroes " and "Hereward

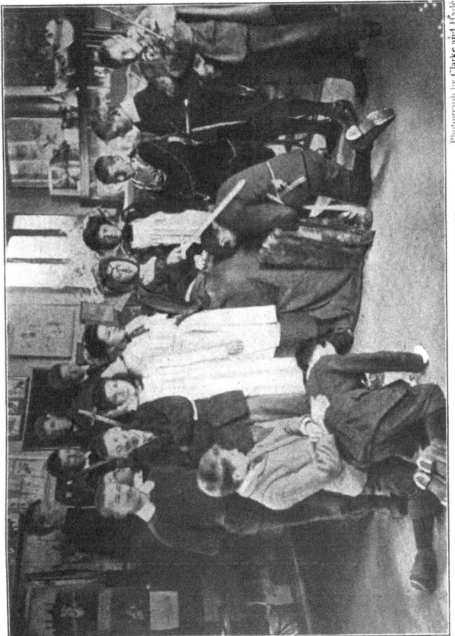

Photograph by Clarke and Hyde

THE KNIGHTING OF RALEIGH

(Note the jealousy of the courtiers)

the Wake," Scott's "Kenilworth," "The Talisman," and "The Abbot," Blackmore's "Lorna Doone"; several good tales of sea adventures of the times of Raleigh, Drake, and Frobisher; as many good histories as we could collect, really good manuals, — a "Green" and a "Fletcher," — all found a place on our shelves. Particularly useful books were collections of stories from the original authorities of history. We had various books which contained stories bearing on every reign, and since these stories were translated or adapted from the best-known authority on each subject, we regarded them as authentic.

These books were left in an easily accessible place with no locked doors, or elaborate cupboards where they might be stored and neglected. Every pupil knew that, as soon as he or she could read, the books might be freely consulted and used for reading, reference, or making notes at any time, either before, after, or during school hours. Our free system of discipline allowed pupils to hold quiet discussions together, — either at the library shelf or at their desks, — and I found the more I trusted them, the more trustworthy and unsuspecting they became. One would see a child quietly get up, walk to the shelf, hunt through the books for a probably useful one on the subject in hand, spend a little quiet time turning the pages, become absorbed, raise his head and say, " Miss Johnson, there is so-and-so in this book!" or " Here's the very thing we want — can't we put this in such-and-such a play?" or take out a notebook, always kept handy, and busily make pencil notes.

There was often quite a rush for the driest of history books, because such books supplied all the facts without too much padding, and were most useful and reliable in tracing the life histories of notable personages. For the same reason biographies were eagerly sought — not because the pupils had been told to study biographies, mark you, but because they had, *for themselves*, discovered their intrinsic value. I cannot too often or too strongly insist on this point; namely, the way in which the dramatic method made the pupils of our school self-reliant, largely self-taught, and self-developing. How many generations of children have turned with disgust and loathing from the dry-as-dust textbook (for examination purposes) — history served up to them in an undigestible mass! I, myself, have been among the number. After all, it makes all the difference in the world how one's food is served up. If it looks attractive and dainty, it is eaten with relish. Just as food enjoyed nourishes the body, so lessons enjoyed are readily assimilated by the mind. Thus instead of turning from the dry textbooks and fact lore, my pupils voluntarily asked for them, and used them well. It was the case over again of the food rendered attractive. Why? Because we had put the textbook *in its proper place* — not as the principal means, but merely as a reference, and for assistance. It has often been argued against our method that it taught the pupils to rely on themselves too much, and on books too little — that the children neglected books too much. The fact is, the basis of all their work was not one book, but many books.

No play was adapted from any one book. All the authorities on the subject of the play were consulted, brought together in note form, and reviewed. The best material was then selected from each, and any hiatus supplied from the intelligent imagination of any member of the class who hit the " public opinion " on the matter. (We were a very united community !)

As soon as the necessary material — or, at least, sufficient to make a fair start — had been collected, the next step was naturally to choose characters, cast parts, and either read the play through or tentatively rehearse. Here, again, our system of freedom of discipline served us in good stead. It did not take very long to discover among the scholars a bold moving spirit. In other circumstances he might have been warped into a ringleader or black sheep. I soon found I had merely to say to him : "John, suppose you take the books and go with the boys out into the playground. I dare say you can all manage to choose your parts. See what sort of a play you can make from what you have collected." In less time than one would think possible, they would be back, tapping on the school-room door, with the play in such a condition that I would be quite astonished at the originality and individuality shown. At the same time one of the most noticeable features was the way in which the pupils, children as they were, would bring out, apparently quite casually and without effort, the salient points of the history they were engaged in *learning* without being taught formally. They showed, too, a marvelous aptitude for casting the right pupils for parts, in which task they were doubtless much aided by John and his successors. No doubt, too, the tone of the school — its new school tradition — helped those who felt they could interpret a part to declare themselves ; and it seemed an unwritten law that any one who volunteered in this way should be given a fair trial, the volunteer always realizing that if he proved unsuitable in the opinion of the majority, he should make way for some one else.

" What happened to the pupils for whom no parts could be found?" I hear you ask. Whenever it was possible, they were worked into a "crowd" of citizens, or an "army," or a "crew"; but where this was out of the question, they sat at their desks and formed a "chorus," whose duty it was to announce players, fill up gaps in the play with explanations, tell dates, and give suggestions. In fact, they were made by every means to feel that they were necessary to and a part of the play, and of course they learned a great deal of history and " English " by listening and commenting, and they were very active at this. All this did away with the idea of "audience" and consequently with " acting for display," self-consciousness, nerves, and possible jealousy and heartburnings, of which, of course, we desired to steer clear.

As regards space, apparatus, properties, and time, we used, when acting in school, merely the ordinary space in front of the class — about twenty feet by six feet, or rather less. A door opening out of it led into the hall, and another door led into the classroom, which could be used in an emergency. We found this especially convenient when,

as often happened, one pupil had to impersonate two characters and needed to make a quick change. Our apparatus
was very simple. It consisted mainly of the school furniture, which I am sure pleased the pupils more than the
most elaborate scenery I could have provided. They simply
howled with delight when " Charles II " was hidden in a
real cupboard — the more so as " Charles " proved to be a
very substantial boy, highly difficult to stow away between
narrow shelves. He comported himself like a true " Royal
Martyr " of the Stuart brand, and endured agonies of
thumpings and pummelings by the anxious actors, who
desired to shut the cupboard door before the " Round-
heads " arrived. Ingenuity decreed, on another occasion,
that " Scrooge " (of Dickens's " Christmas Carol " fame)
should look out of a window consisting of the top of a
blackboard easel with a movable rail for hanging diagrams
before the class. This scheme was enjoyed tremendously,
and the inventor was loudly praised. This was a most
noticeable outcome of the method of work : pupils would
always praise good work in others, and if their companions appeared unnoticed when praise was due, they drew
attention to what they had done.

When reading, a short while ago, Richard Jefferies's
book " Bevis," I came across the following paragraph,[1]
which emphasizes very strongly my plea for self-made
and self-planned properties : " He knew that the greatest
pleasure is always obtained from inferior and incomplete
instruments. Present a perfect yacht, a beautiful horse, a

[1] P. 217.

fine gun, or anything complete to a beginner, and the edge of his enjoyment is dulled with too speedy possession. The best way to learn to ride is on a rough pony."

The boys, of course, always enjoyed battle scenes, and made different "properties" for use in different battles, in order that the various reigns and periods might not be confused. Thus for early English times they manufactured halberds, or "brown bills," out of cardboard (for the metal work) and broom handles. Big brothers and fathers at home became interested at this point, and "properties" which were well worth preserving for future use began to come in to us so fast that we had to set up a cupboard

for storing them. Thus one father made a beautiful brass crown inset with colored glass jewels. Several persons presented us with wooden swords — the blades were silvered, and generally the handles were of bent tin and had some little realistic touch. An older brother carved and contrived some daggers in sheaths. Again, in this instance, the design had been faithfully copied from a history; the carver was a former pupil of the school, who still kept up his interest. In planning our armies we always found out from the histories the real numbers on each side, and kept ours as nearly as possible in proportion. Thus in "Agincourt" we ranged our English and French seven to one. In the trial of Charles I we arranged that the court should contain six men to represent sixty, and the "chorus" always told us that there were sixty men present.

Sea maneuvers were popular, and we refought many a battle between English and Dutch. For these I allowed the boys to bring their soap boxes on wheels, generally

preferring those with guiding wheels in front. It was great fun when the boys maneuvered into position (after many capsizings and accidents) with their cannon and fire-arms on board. Once the Dutch leader had his box boat turned into the semblance of a real ship by covering it with cardboard over a cane-work skeleton, and rigging masts and sails of paper. To add the realistic touch each boy had plenty of chains on his boat to rattle when he dropped or weighed anchor. The next morning, long before nine o'clock, I surprised all the first-class boys with heads together over a history with illustrations, looking up material for another bout with Van Tromp. The soap boxes on wheels (cube-sugar boxes too, sometimes) were one of our most valuable assets. The boys picked the wheels up from ragmen or marine stores for a few cents each, and found them very handy in their own little gardens, using the boxes as wheelbarrows. Anon they did duty for ships on voyages of discovery to other lands, and were very skillfully manipulated past dangerous shores, where desks — I mean *capes* — projected. "Queen Elizabeth's" state barge was a soap box — on this occasion draped in red cloth. If no soap box was available on history day, however, no one was at a loss, for a bench, inverted, was slowly and gracefully dragged across the floor with "her Majesty" seated thereon. "Charles II" escaped to France in a disused bathtub, which rocked beautifully. From the same tub fishermen on the Volga hooked giant "fish" in the shape of the school dusters. One of the most comical properties was a set of brown-paper animals' skins, into which small boys would creep, and add a very realistic touch to geography and other plays. "John," before mentioned, designed and painted these, and the girls sewed them up. Another ingenious boy cut a suit of Saxon serf's garments out of sacking and sewed them at home

by himself. The girls, of course, could do much in making costumes, and we soon found that certain stock garments were wanted which could be used for most history
plays. These, of course, saved the trouble of making fresh
costumes every time. For instance, there was generally a
king, and of course he would wear a crimson cloak trimmed
with ermine (wadding painted with dots of ink) and a
crown. A scepter was made by a father out of a brass
bedpost cut short. It was useful also to have a bishop's
miter of brown paper covered with gold paper. Queen's
and court ladies' robes were fashioned of white lace window curtains pinned at the shoulders and allowed to trail.
A court jester's cap and bells were easy to make. A few
pairs of sateen knickerbockers and short cloaks were made
by the girls from patterns supplied by a pupil's mother,
and these could be adapted to many periods. Coarse string
or knitting cotton made up into "shirts of mail" was dyed
with ink and afterwards touched up with silver paint to
give a tarnished metal appearance. Womens' discarded
black stockings made long "trunk hose" for the boys. A
crowning triumph was the fashioning, by the girls, of naval
officers' coats, for use by "Nelson" and his officers, out
of old black and navy blue skirts, with large silver-papered
buttons. True, "Hardy" soon grew out of *his* coat, and
looked as funny as a Cruikshank illustration, with his waist
buttons halfway up his back and his wristbands almost at
his elbows.

The tea-paper armor was always mounted on either
stout brown paper or cardboard, so that it should not

become ragged. We found ordinary paper fasteners suitable for joints, and where it was possible to use them they were more serviceable than stitches. Paper fasteners also made very effective "studs" for shields, and the most successful costume we ever made was one for Edward when we played "The Burghers of Calais." We cut out a large shield in cardboard and bent it slightly. This we covered carefully with white cartridge paper, overlapping the paper at the edges and attaching it to the cardboard with brass paper fasteners as "studs." Next we cut out the royal arms of England in gold paper and carefully pasted them on the shield. We then made Edward a cloak of white cotton cloth and bordered it with gold paper. Our method of fastening gold paper to this cloth was our own, and we found it practicable. We mixed a tablespoonful of starch with boiling water, and when it cooled applied it to the back of our strips and patterns of gold paper. These we laid carefully in position on the cloth and then ironed them flat with a hot flatiron. The patterns then looked as though they had been painted or embroidered on the garment. This form of decoration was easy and effective, and looked especially well when the golden fleur-de-lis was used as the pattern for bordering. Odd strings of beads given by the pupils from time to time answered for "jewels," and our armory included some homemade bows and arrows. These articles were all kept in one cupboard, duly labeled, ready for immediate use, and were looked upon in the light of school apparatus as much as sets of historical readers or piles of slates; and we considered them no more trouble to attend to and keep tidy. We found that children of the upper classes were generally of a fairly uniform size, and we always renewed such things as paper headgear when a new actor had to take a certain part, so that there should be no danger of infection.

We tried, when possible, to arrange that the boy who had once been a king should not be another king — at all events during the same school year. We hoped in this way to avoid confusion of reigns in the pupils' minds. We treated all important personages, such as Nelson, in the same way.

The time occupied by history *plays* proper consisted of that set apart for history *lessons*, because we considered our play in the light of a lesson. We had two of these each week, one of a half hour's duration, and one of one hour. Preparation had to occupy the pupils' own leisure time and odd minutes in school, many of which would otherwise have been wasted ; while for the making of notes an occasional writing lesson was set apart. Once a week we had what we termed a "library morning," when each pupil was allowed to take a book from the library shelf and read it silently at his desk. Questions might be asked and answered, and little discussions were permitted, so long as only one person spoke at a time and the general order and quiet of the class was not upset too much. Then it was that the most valuable discoveries were made for possible "plays," and a good deal of the preparation done.

Frequently, too, while on an expedition or "nature ramble" in the summer time, we would be out of doors the whole morning. Then when the ordinary playtime arrived we would arrange ourselves on the side of the downs or in a little copse, and go through a short history play; occasionally we would arrange a new and impromptu one. Sometimes these were very well arranged by the children; often they were better, from an educational standpoint, than plays to which more preparation had been given. At the time of the Quebec pageant in memory of the gallant Wolfe, the boys arranged a most successful and thrilling "Wolfe on the Heights of Abraham" in a disused chalk pit, where they could scale the heights most realistically. And of course Charles II and the Boscobel Oak episode could be played to perfection only in a little wooded plantation. Scenes from their favorite "Ivanhoe" were the delight of their hearts on summer afternoons under the shade of the greenwood tree.

And here, in passing, as an example of how this kind of teaching was training the pupils to a sense of the fitness of things (a splendid possession through life!), I ought to mention that they soon began to quote from good authors quite appropriately and naturally. On the first occasion on which they tried scenes from "Ivanhoe," out in the little wooded spot, they naturally connected their Locksley or Robin Hood and his bold outlaws with the greenwood tree, and needs must pose themselves like a band of "merry men" enjoying an evening rest, while an unseen chorus of girls behind the trees sang "Under the Greenwood Tree," to Dr. Arne's setting. A finer effect I have never heard from the most practiced of singers, the

voices mellowed by the open air — young, fresh voices —
and the birds in the trees overhead echoing and vying
with their song! After all, *why do we sing?* To please
the sense of hearing, and also a deeper, more æsthetic
sense. Then our children should learn to sing artistically
and in the open air. And *does* the ordinary school singing
please the senses? Does it not lack spontaneity? Then
let your pupils use their singing for a purpose, and you
will find that they will realize what is required instinctively
and supply the effect. I called this little tableau "dramatizing" their singing. Some may question the effect on
the listeners. What I saw was a group of silent, thoughtful-
looking boys, resting in perfectly natural poses, and sobered
in spite of their youth and boisterous, boyish spirits, to a
quiet, listening attitude. I have not the faintest doubt that
theirs was perfect enjoyment, for the spell was not broken
when the song ceased. I did not question them as to
their sensations, nor ask if they enjoyed the music, nor
what their impressions of it were. I doubt if they could
have told me in so many words. But they have often,
since then, asked to have the song again in school, and
the boys have always supplied the soft whistling of the birds
as an accompaniment because the real birds were missing.

CHAPTER III

THE ADAPTED PLAY

AS an example of what I may call an "adapted" play, and more particularly one for girls as well as boys, I give that on the reign of Elizabeth, as it was partly adapted from "Kenilworth" and partly originated by individual scholars. It is copied from one of the girls' notebooks. The boys had fixed up the movable blackboard table as a tobacco stall; other stalls were arranged on the front desks; while the space in front was supposed to represent a street in old London — the chorus generally said Cheapside. All those taking part in the play were ranged at one end of the room, which we called "off stage." Those left seated in the desks and called "chorus" then described the scene as they imagined it to be — narrow streets badly paved with cobblestones, stalls with market women keeping them and calling their wares, and idle apprentices.

SCENE I. *The Market*

Enter two Market Women *with baskets of wares.* Apprentices *scattered about the stalls, calling,* "What d'ye lack?"

FIRST WOMAN. Hast heard the news that Philip hath sent a large fleet of ships to England against us?

44

THE COLLAPSE OF MRS. MICAWBER WHEN SHE SEES DAVID COPPERFIELD AFTER HER RETURN

45

SECOND WOMAN. Odds, woman! thou dost surprise me.

FIRST WOMAN. There are hundreds and hundreds of them, and I did hear that a man named Drake and some of his friends were playing at bowls down at Plymouth Hoe, when another man came riding up to them and told them that the Spanish were in the Channel. The good Queen, God bless her! went down to see the army, riding on her gray pony.

Enter Third Market Woman, *while a* Man *draws near to listen, eating a large apple*

THIRD WOMAN. Do you know that the English are sending out fire ships?

SECOND WOMAN. Lawk-a-mussey-me! What are they?

THIRD WOMAN. Why, they are old vessels filled with tar, and gunpowder, and things that will burn easily. They turn these adrift among the enemy's ships and they either set fire to the other ships or blow them up.

SECOND WOMAN. They say the Spanish ships sail in a half-moon shape.

MAN. [*With apple*] Ah, it wants stout English hearts like mine to fight the Spaniards!

FIRST WOMAN. Methinks your stomach is greater than your heart.

SECOND WOMAN. Yes, judging by the size of his apple —but hark! here comes the Queen. We must be off to our stalls.

Enter QUEEN ELIZABETH, Court Ladies, *and* Courtiers

MARKET WOMEN. What d'ye lack? What d'ye lack?

FIRST WOMAN. [*Curtsies*] Ribbons and laces for sweet pretty faces, your Majesty!

FIRST COURT LADY. I will have a yard of sarcenet to deck my bodice for this evening's morris dance.

SECOND WOMAN. Nice, fresh arum roots to stiffen the ladies' ruffles, your Majesty!

QUEEN. Yes, my ruffles are exceedingly limp. I will have a pound sent to the palace.

THIRD WOMAN. Woundwort, to cure cuts and bruises, your Majesty!

COURT LADY. Oh, your Majesty, do you not remember that poor soldier who was wounded in a bout at quarter-staff last night?

QUEEN. Indeed, poor fellow! then see that he has some woundwort made into poultices and applied to his sore pate.

THIRD WOMAN. Stitchwort, to cure stitch in the side, your Majesty!

SECOND WOMAN. Rosemary and thyme to scent the floors with, your Majesty!

COURT LADY. See, your Majesty, the new flower called wallflower, brought from America!

QUEEN. Methinks I should like to smell that sweet flower. [Market Woman *presents a bunch, which the* QUEEN *sniffs daintily. They pass along until they reach tobacco stall*] See, my ladies, the new stuff called tobacco,

COMBAT BETWEEN RODERICK DHU AND FITZ-JAMES

49

brought from Virginia! [Courtiers *stop and purchase cigars and awkwardly light them; the* QUEEN *meanwhile passes on a few steps*] Oh, this muddy pool — what shall we do, my ladies? And my feet are so lightly shod! [WALTER RALEIGH *steps forward and gracefully places the cloak which he has worn lightly on his shoulders over the muddy spot — remaining kneeling on one knee while the* Ladies, *headed by the* QUEEN, *pass over dry-shod*] Who is that young courtier?

FIRST COURT LADY. He is one Walter Raleigh, your Majesty, who sailed the oceans wide, and brought back the tobacco, and the potato, and the wallflower from Virginia.

SECOND COURT LADY. And called it Virginia after the Virgin Queen, your Majesty.

QUEEN. Well, bring him to the palace, and perhaps we shall find him a post there. Now to the barge, my ladies.

[*Exeunt all slowly*]

The words of this scene the children obtained from various sources, and invented all they could not so obtain. It was characteristic of them that they worked in a little of their nature study when they alluded to "woundwort," "stitchwort," and "arum roots." It is a fact that wild arum (cuckoopint) tubers contain starch, which was used for starching ruffs in Elizabeth's reign. The children discovered the starch by applying iodine and obtaining a purple-colored reaction.

The children next changed the scene to Kenilworth
Castle, and borrowed the wording of their scene from
Sir Walter Scott's "Kenilworth."

SCENE II. *Kenilworth Castle, described by* Chorus
as usual

Music — something stately — generally a gavotte. Courtiers *and* Ladies *enter, a few at a time. The various
groups greet one another with profound, courtly bows
and the deepest of curtsies. Music grows louder and
imitates fanfare of trumpets. Enter* QUEEN. *The*
Courtiers *and* Ladies *fall back into two lines, and the*
QUEEN *bows from side to side. Her* Ladies *accompany
her, and* Pages *carry her train.* QUEEN *sits down,
and all the* Ladies *and* Gentlemen *group themselves
about her*

QUEEN. Bring in that young courtier.
COURTIER. Yes, your Majesty. [*Goes out, bowing. His
voice is then heard*] The Queen requires you in her
presence.

Enter RALEIGH. *He kneels in front of the* QUEEN

QUEEN. You have, young man, spoilt a gay mantle in
our service. We thank you for your courtesy, but your
gallantry shall not go unrewarded. Go to the wardrobe
keeper and he shall supply you with a suit quite of

A PART OF THE "CHRISTMAS CAROL" FESTIVAL

53

the latest cut. [RALEIGH *shakes his head and makes a sign as if he declined the* QUEEN'S *present*] How now, boy? What wouldst thou have of me — neither gold nor garment?

RALEIGH. Only permission, madam, to wear my own cloak.

QUEEN. To wear thine own muddy cloak, thou silly boy! Heard ye ever the likes, my lords?

RALEIGH. It is no longer my cloak, since your Majesty's foot hath trodden upon it.

QUEEN. Then we will reward you in our own way. Your sword, Essex. [*The* EARL *kneels and hands his sword to the* QUEEN, *who strikes* RALEIGH *lightly over the shoulder with it*] Rise, *Sir* Walter Raleigh. [RALEIGH *rises gracefully, while the other* Courtiers *show jealousy and look displeased*]

ESSEX. Will you knight *my* friend, Nicholas Blount, your Majesty?

QUEEN. Yes — bring him in. [BLOUNT *is fetched*] Your sword, Essex! Rise, Sir Nicholas Blount! [*He rises awkwardly and clutches at the* QUEEN *to save himself*]

FIRST COURT LADY. Did you see how awkwardly he arose, your Majesty?

SECOND COURT LADY. I heard his collar bone rattle.

QUEEN. [*Laughing*] Yes, I did give him a smart tap. Now we will have a dance. [*They dance a stately measure*] Now to the banquet — your arm, Essex. [*Exeunt all*]

CHAPTER IV

THE ORIGINAL PLAY

A SLIGHTLY different kind of play I have termed the *original* play. In arranging these the pupils themselves collected all the material from histories proper, and did not in any way rely on works of fiction or the historical novel or storybook for their dialogue. Naturally, as they were acting history, they had to get facts from some record in the same way as an ordinary dramatist must do. Therefore they consulted the historians but not the writers of fiction. This kind of play was consequently more difficult to get in form than such a play as " Elizabeth," in which much of the dialogue was taken directly from books. One of the most successful of these " original " historical plays was that called " Charles I." For this the pupils chose six boys to be dressed as Puritans and represent sixty, ranged on seats in the usual front space, now called by the chorus Westminster Hall. Each boy wore a tall stovepipe hat of brown paper (made by the girls and painted black with ink) to show that he was a Puritan. As the class agreed that the Puritans should be stern men, the sort of men to " stand no nonsense," each boy was always careful to wear a very sober, not to say stern, visage. The way in which they preserved their gravity

56

was quite marvelous—in fact, they were so much "in the play," heart and soul, that they did not think of anything but the proper demeanor. Other characters chosen were "Bradshaw," the judge, in his famous black hat, which the girls also constructed, making it extra large to distinguish him from the others; "Cromwell," wearing a sword to distinguish him as the head of the Ironsides; "Coke," the clerk of the court, wearing robes (sheets), and holding a scroll of paper (from which, by the way, he read his part to save learning it by heart at first); "Charles I," wearing a curled wig, which deserves a paragraph all to itself.

It was designed and made by one of the older girls. She made the foundation by crocheting a skull cap of wool, and to this she sewed strands of frayed rope which looked like fine glossy hair. When she reached this stage it was tried on a boy's head and given a "hair cut" to make the ends even. Then the "hair" was carefully curled in papers and pressed, after which it looked like a Cavalier's curled wig.

"Charles" also wore very debonairly a black velvet "picture" hat, given by a friend. We "corked" his mustache and short beard. He wore a pair of the sateen knickerbockers and the long stockings before alluded to, a sword, a graceful cloak (made out of a woman's skirt), buckled shoes, and carried a knobbed stick which, as it had to do duty in the play, had the knob previously loosened so that it would fall off easily. Other Cavaliers who accompanied him also had wigs, knickerbockers, and swords. The

" plumes " in their hats were novel, consisting merely of sprays of pampas grass such as are used in vases for decorative purposes. The girls were dressed in window curtains, with long trains, and carried fans (of plaited paper). Their hair and headdresses were copied from pictures of the period and were arranged before school time. The boy who acted as Coke in the first scenes took the part of Bishop Juxon in the later scenes, because, as he was already draped in " robes," all he had to do to show that he was a bishop was to don a miter. The two young children of Charles, the Duke of Gloucester and little Princess Elizabeth, were dressed as nearly as possible like the pictures one sees of them, and were chosen from the small children, so as not to make the " father " look ridiculous. " Princess Elizabeth " wore a close-fitting lace cap and had two tiny pages to walk behind her. The boys drew and painted a coat of arms to take the place of the royal arms of England, bearing the words " God with us." This they pinned on the cupboard door, where " Charles " could not fail to see it on entering. For the king they placed the high desk chair, so that he might be in a prominent position.

The first scene was laid in Westminster Hall and represented the " first day's trial." The chorus always informed us that after the first day's trial we skipped over to the seventh day's trial. Here is the play as copied from a pupil's notebook, with comments by me.

LITTLE RED RIDING-HOOD

SCENE I. *Westminster Hall*

Enter Gentlemen of the Court. *When all are assembled, enter* CROMWELL

CROMWELL. Sirs, we have met here to-day to try a certain man named Charles Stuart, who has done much harm to this country. We have had enough of his tyrannies, his Star Chambers, and his illegal ways of getting money. This *must* be stopped.

PURITANS. Yes, it must!

CROMWELL. He has been taught by his father the divine right of kings, and by the evil influence of the Duke of Buckinghamshire, helped on by his wife, he has caused the blood of many thousands to be shed.

COKE. Yes, his evil influence has had a great effect.

CROMWELL. It must be stopped. We must cut these Stuarts out, root and branch.

Enter BRADSHAW

BRADSHAW. As we have met here to-day to try this man named Charles Stuart, go and fetch the prisoner.

[Ushers of the Court *go out and reënter, followed by* KING CHARLES, *accompanied by* COLONEL HACKER *and other* Cavaliers]

BRADSHAW. Clerk, read the charge.

COKE. [*Reads*] The charge stateth that, with limited power to govern according to law, you should use that power for the benefit of the people — their rights, and liberties. But you have tried to take away the remedy for misgovernment, and in making war on the present Parliament you have caused the blood of many thousands to be shed. All this is against the public interest and common rights, liberty, justice, and peace of the people of this nation. You are a tyrant and a traitor!

CHARLES. Hold! hold! [*He touches* COKE *on the shoulder with his cane. The head of the cane drops off and rolls away. No one stirs to pick it up, although* CHARLES *looks round for them to do so. He picks it up himself*]

BRADSHAW. Remove the prisoner. [CHARLES *is removed, looking scornfully around*]

CHORUS. End of first day's trial.

SCENE II. *Westminster Hall six days afterwards*

Enter Gentlemen, Ushers, *&c., as before. The* Gentlemen *talk in undertones and seem to discuss the trial very gravely. Enter* CROMWELL

CROMWELL. Have you agreed on your verdict, gentlemen?

JURYMAN. Yes, we have.

CROMWELL. What shall it be?

JURYMAN. Execution.

CROMWELL. When it is done it cannot be undone, so decide carefully, gentlemen.

JURYMAN. There is no other way. It *must* be done.

Enter BRADSHAW

BRADSHAW. Have you decided on your verdict, gentlemen? What shall it be?

JURYMEN. Execution! execution!

CROMWELL. Come, we will sign his death warrant.

[*The warrant is signed, sealed, and stamped with the great seal of England.* COKE *holds it out to view*]

COKE. Will this suit your wishes, gentlemen?

JURYMEN. Yes.

BRADSHAW. Go and fetch the prisoner.

[*They make their way to the court. The* Crowd (*represented by the* Chorus *in desks, with a few standing*) *form two lines*]

CROWD. Justice! justice! Execution! execution!

SOLDIER. [*Steps forward as* CHARLES *passes*] God bless you, your Majesty! [*The* KING *thanks him, but an* Officer *strikes the* Soldier *with his cane*]

CHARLES. Methinks that the punishment was greater than the offense. [*He turns to the* Cavalier *walking beside him*] Did you hear that cry for justice?

CAVALIER. Yes, your Majesty, and I wondered at it.

CHARLES. So do not I. They will do anything their officer tells them, and they would say the same thing to their officers, if there were occasion, to-morrow. [*They enter the court*]

CHARLES. [*Looking at the coat of arms*] God with us! Do you see that coat of arms?

COLONEL HACKER. Yes, it is the wrong one! [CHARLES *glances round the court, sits down, and then starts up again*]

BRADSHAW. Clerk, read the sentence.

CHARLES. I refuse to be tried by this court! Where are the peers, who, by the laws of England, alone can try me?

BRADSHAW. *We* will try you! Clerk, read the sentence.

COKE. [*Reads*] Hear the appointment and purpose of this High Court which the king hath refused to acknowledge. The sentence which you are about to hear is the act and judgment of this High Court. The charge is proved upon you as the principal culprit, for all of which treasons and crimes this court doth adjudge that Charles Stuart is a traitor, murderer, a liar —

LADY FAIRFAX. It's a lie!

USHER. Who spoke there?

LADY FAIRFAX. I spoke.

USHER. Silence in the court!

BRADSHAW. Proceed.

COKE. I repeat, is a traitor, murderer, a liar, and a public enemy, and shall be put to death by severing his head from his body.

BRADSHAW. The sentence which you have heard is the act, sentence, judgment, and resolution of the whole court. Remove the prisoner.

CHARLES. [*Starting up*] But, sir, I may speak after the sentence.

BRADSHAW. Sir, you are not to be heard after the sentence.

CHARLES. [*Much agitated*] I may speak after the sentence! Always, by your favor, sir! I may speak after the sentence — by your favor —

BRADSHAW. Hold!

CHARLES. [*Being led from court*] They will not let me speak — they will not let me speak!

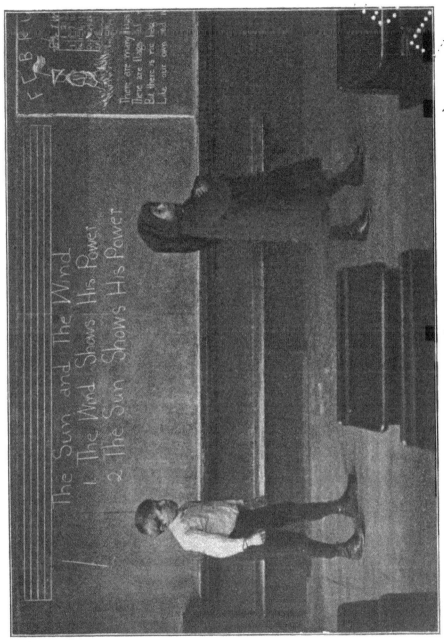

THE SUN AND THE WIND (THE WIND SHOWS HIS POWER)

SCENE III. *A room in Whitehall*

CHARLES *is seated, with* BISHOP JUXON, COLONEL HACKER, COLONEL TOMLINSON, *and* SIR THOMAS HERBERT *standing near*

CHARLES. I should like to see my children.

BISHOP JUXON. Yes, your Majesty. [*He goes out. Reënter* BISHOP JUXON *with* PRINCESS ELIZABETH *and young* DUKE OF GLOUCESTER]

CHARLES. They are going to cut off thy father's head, my children.

CHILDREN. Oh, father! father!

DUKE OF GLOUCESTER. Do not let them cut off my father's head!

CHARLES. They will cut off thy brothers' heads if they catch them. Do not you ever be a king, my son, or they will cut off thy head also.

DUKE OF GLOUCESTER. I will be torn in pieces first.

CHARLES. Give my love to your mother.

CHILDREN. Yes, father.

CHARLES. Farewell, my children!

CHILDREN. Oh, father! father! [*They are led out, sobbing, by* BISHOP JUXON. CHARLES *falls on his knees, and the three others do the same. The bell tolls. They rise, and* JUXON *lays his hand on* CHARLES's *shoulder*]

BISHOP JUXON. You have only one stage more. It is troublesome, but short. It will carry you from earth to heaven. God bless you, your Majesty!

CHARLES. It will carry me from an earthly crown to a heavenly one. Farewell! [*To* HERBERT] Take my sword. [*To* JUXON] Take my watch. [*The bell tolls*]

I could not help being struck by the manner in which the children had collaborated to bring out the points of the history they desired to learn and teach, — just those points which a teacher would probably note down as the things necessary to emphasize, — and yet it was all done without effort. No doubt the reason was that each actor had his mind so much on his own part, and was so much in the part, that he was thoroughly acquainted with all the " whys " and the " wherefores," and with causes and their results. An ordinary class of children sitting still at desks, feeling themselves to be merely *a class* of children, might or might not be interested enough to inquire for reasons or results of actions. It is doubtful whether they would remember even what they heard, except for a very short time. Teachers have constantly to devise plans for insuring that children not only listen and pay attention but also remember what they hear. The truth is, that we all remember what we actually *see* and *do* better than what we merely hear — perhaps force ourselves to hear or are forced to hear.

I wonder if people ever reflect on the enormous number of facts which are talked *into* children in elementary schools for probably seven whole consecutive years ! How monotonous it must become, although the child may not realize that it is monotony ! Why should it be considered

THE SUN AND THE WIND (THE SUN SHOWS HIS POWER)

so virtuous a thing for a class of children to sit still and listen, while a teacher (who is probably often very tired of it) talks on every subject or adopts what I call the " stand-and-deliver " attitude, and demands from the children opinions which they have not, as yet, formed! The whole lecture and question-and-answer system appears to me now to be so dead — so utterly devoid of life! If we are anxious to obtain a child's opinions and to find out what he really knows (and consequently will remember), we should confront him with what he may be expected to be able to assimilate, and should throw the whole responsibility of as-similation onto him; in other words, *it is useless to eat the child's food for him; he must eat it himself*. To lec-ture a child on a certain subject and then to ask him one or two questions on it does not prove that he has learned, knows, or will remember anything about it. He may make a clever shot at the answer or he may be a little " parrot." And how much useless lumber we may pack into a child's mind in seven years of "fact teaching!" For instance, of what practical value is it for a boy to know that Charles I was executed and said certain words at his trial, and to know the number of men who tried him, their names, and the dates when such things took place? It may not be the facts themselves which are so valuable; it is the *habit of mind* formed while learning them which makes their worth. If a boy has to search out the facts for himself, for a pleas-urable object, he will probably do it thoroughly; and while doing so he will exercise his ingenuity, resourcefulness, self-reliance, and intelligence. If he does not exercise these powers, it is certain, by the laws of nature, that they will become attenuated for want of use or be lost altogether. And I have heard frequent complaints from teachers that "So-and-so, who used to be so very bright in the primary school, seems to have lost all intelligence and is quite dull in the simplest things."

There have been rumors, too, in other quarters, that boys leaving school and beginning work are lacking in initiative and self-reliance — both "business" qualities needed by boys. There is only one way to develop self-reliance and initiative, and that is to exercise these powers. If boys are expected to show signs of possessing these qualities on leaving school, then the time to develop and exercise them is *in* school. There are not many ways in which such powers can be exercised while the pupils remain grouped in classes. It often happens that individual work cannot be done in class. But I have found that my dramatic method forced children to develop and exercise these powers automatically.

A glance at the foregoing play will illustrate my remarks. The boy who represented Cromwell had to write his own speeches, and therefore on *him* was thrown the responsibility of finding out and putting together material. This was the first step toward developing self-reliance—responsibility of the individual. Probably one book of reference failed him and he developed *perseverance*. All books failed him at some junctures and he had to display *ingenuity*. He had to work in an introduction to the play and its characters, and in a few words describe the hero indirectly

yet gracefully. Here came in *resourcefulness*. Glance at
his first speech and see how he accomplished all this without being talked into it or questioned out of it. He first ex-
plains why the Puritans are assembled. He introduces the
hero by name. He gives the Puritan version of Charles's
character, the reasons for disliking him. He enumerates
the crimes attributed to him or hints at them briefly. He
finds reasons for Charles's weakness of character, — "he
has been taught by his father," etc., — so he had evidently
hunted up the reign of James I to find causes. This is
not only teaching composition, but, at the same time,
inculcating important habits of mind. After all, of what
use is it to teach a child to write a fair composition if the
other habits of mind are lacking or only survive in spite
of circumstances? In planning his speech he evidently
conferred with "Coke," because the next long and explan-
atory speech is by the boy representing Coke, who realizes
that his opportunity lies in enumerating in greater detail
the faults of Charles. "Cromwell" realized that he might
properly be brief and leave detail to "Coke." Here was
forethought. And here were two schoolboys *analyzing*
history and men! Is it not worth a trial, this method
which has such results to show?

After all, it did not need much resourcefulness, self-
reliance, or initiative to reproduce a story which had been
read aloud to the class twice, or to write a page of "composition" on a given subject, particularly when actual
"headings" of the various sections of it were written on
the blackboard for compulsory use! I have read many

pathetic attempts of young pupils to oblige the autocrat who dictated these "headings," and I have heard of one poor little boy who tried to write an essay on the "cat," using "orange" headings, with disastrous results; for he wrote: "The skin of the cat is its fur" (that was under the heading "skin"). "Its flesh is the pulp. Its seeds I do not know." I do not think I ever found the children of my school writing about something they did not understand, because a child generally knows a great deal about what he "plays"; and also because the pupils had formed a habit of freely discussing and "threshing out" difficulties with the community, in the act of doing which they deepened the impressions made on their brains, making remembrance more easy.

It may have already occurred to the reader that one effect of the play — more particularly the original play — on the children would necessarily be a great improvement in their speech and diction. They naturally learned to speak freely, to enunciate clearly, and to avoid mumbling or chattering. They learned to choose their phrases carefully and to clothe their thoughts in appropriate words. To give an instance of what I mean: one little girl was telling me that she had planted some seeds. She said, "I planted them in some dirt in a box." Another small child immediately said, "Don't say 'dirt,' say 'mold' or 'earth.'" Young as she was, she had learned to differentiate between the polite term and the reverse. On another occasion, while on a nature ramble with the older pupils, I was picking my way over a very rough road full of old wagon ruts which had cut deeply into the soil. We were walking single file to avoid the mud. I turned to the girl immediately behind me and said: "This is a horrid road." "'Alas! my journey, rugged and uneven,'" quoted she.

It was a great help to the children, in learning to speak correctly, to be allowed to use appropriate and natural gesture, as was possible while acting a part. One remembers the "actions" taught in lessons set apart for "recitation" and "action songs." How little they expressed what the child himself felt! And how impossible it was to show any real "expression" or feeling when reciting with the hands held rigidly behind the back!

It is true that the chorus of pupils who had no speaking parts had to sit at their desks during the performance of plays, but a great measure of the success of a play depended on them. Even they had no set form of words dictated to them. They were told to find words for themselves, and not a little of the work fell on them. It is not possible or necessary to act the whole of any reign when playing history. The pupils ingeniously worked into their speeches as much explanation as could be included without being tedious. The rest they left to the chorus, who were constantly on the watch to "put in their oar" when some gap needed filling. For instance, in the play "Charles I" they always explained why the wife and two elder sons of Charles were not near him at his trial. Directly after the first scene, and while the next was being prepared, they would depute one of their number to be spokesman, who would say: "His wife has gone to the continent to try to raise an army," or other words to that effect.

A glance round the school when a "play" was in progress would soon show that all the children there were equally animated, eager, and interested, simply because we were using for educational purposes one of the strongest instincts of childhood, I might almost say of human nature, — we were harnessing another Niagara Falls.

CHAPTER V

THE SHAKESPEAREAN PLAY

IT was only to be expected that, as soon as the pupils of the school had tried to write their own historical plays (and hence knew the points of a good play), they should soon be on the watch for good ready-made plays illustrating the periods they happened to be studying. Naturally they found these in the works of Shakespeare, and thus, as with poetry, songs, and music, they "discovered" Shakespeare's works for themselves. It was not a case of the teacher telling the children to read so-and-so; but, on the contrary, it was the children who drew the teacher's attention to the fact that, in the volume of Shakespeare which they kept on their library shelf, there were good plays which they could act. It was the pupils themselves, too, by the way, who subscribed their pennies and bought a well-illustrated edition of Shakespeare's works, which soon came to be one of the most used books in their library.

Of course, just at first they found the complete plays too lengthy for their purpose and the wording too difficult. Then, once more, their ingenuity came to their aid and they discovered how to abridge and adapt Shakespeare to their own use. They began with "Henry V."

77

Their opening scene showed Henry as the hot-headed young prince, with his boon companions, bragging of the way he had defied Judge Gascoigne. His companions encouraged him, and he, in turn, promised them great honors when he should become king. Suddenly a messenger appears and tells him of the death of the king. He waves off his companions, saying, "Away with you all! I have no more to do with you." The boys liked the first scene tremendously. They quite understood the spirit of the thing and introduced a bit of swordplay and a quarrel, to which young "Prince Hal" put an end by striking up the swords of the combatants.

After this they followed the plan of Shakespeare's "Henry V," made the second scene of that play their first scene, and abridged the "Archbishop of Canterbury's" speeches sufficiently to allow an explanation of Henry's claim to the French throne and his views on the Salic law. It was certainly interesting to watch how cleverly they got over the difficulty of knowing nothing of the French language. They made the messenger from the dauphin speak broken English! The incident of the present of tennis balls was included, and "Henry" was quite fine in his denunciation of the insult and in his determination to send the tennis balls back as "cannon balls."

The chorus in this play next recited from memory the passage from the play beginning

> Now all the youth of England are on fire,
> And silken dalliance in the wardrobe lies,

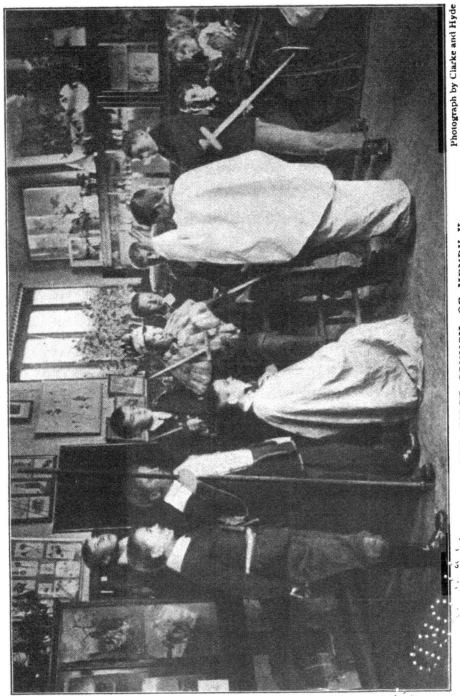

THE FIRST COUNCIL OF HENRY V
(The Archbishop of Canterbury is speaking)

while the king and others donned all the gorgeous armor they could muster. This in most cases consisted of string "chain mail" and silver tea paper. "Henry V" himself wore a shirt of fine mail consisting of a lady's silk vest! Over the headpieces of chain mail they wore helmets, and the principals rode "steeds." They were generally dressed before the chorus had finished reciting, and would then ride past the school window, shaking their "lances" to show they were off to Southampton! Next they fitted in a little scene showing Southampton, the guilty Lords Scroop, Cambridge, and Grey, and their punishment by Henry. Mere writing cannot make my readers realize how well these little rural boys "lived" the parts. The dignity and restraint of "Henry" as he led up to the charge and sentence; the guilty starts and shamed demeanor of the culprits; the correct bearing of "Exeter" as he said, "I arrest thee," etc.; the way in which the last-arrested conspirator broke his sword before delivering it up, were all realistic in the extreme, and certainly had their share in improving the tone and bearing of the boys.

It was in this play that we instituted the rule that when, in a battle scene, the bell was rung, every one should stand quite still in a sort of tableau. This was to guard against accidents. I could stop the "fight" at will. The scene showing the siege of Harfleur was worked in this way: the walls were represented by chairs placed along the side of "stage" space. When "Henry" desired the moment of victory to arrive, he jumped upon one of the chairs, crying, "To the breach! To the breach!" I would then sound the bell and every one struck an attitude just where he was — some "dead," some engaging in combat. The scenes in both camps before the battle of Agincourt were well adapted. The girls always pulled down the blinds to show that it was night; the chorus described the place, time, geographical position, numbers on each side; and "Henry" recited the speech which answers "Westmoreland" when he wished for "one ten thousand of the men of England who do no work to-day."

Of course they had a beautiful tableau for the finish of Agincourt, with both French and English leaders included. The boys suggested a voyage home with French prisoners, and cube-sugar boxes rigged as boats were brought into requisition. All the chorus stood on the seats for a good view of the procession through London, and so real was it to them that I have heard little girls whisper excitedly, "Here they come! Here they come!" and almost fall off the seats craning their necks and waving their handkerchiefs. It was easy to distinguish who were prisoners and who were victors. The former hung their heads and dragged their feet, while the latter held their heads erect and looked triumphant.

The "crowd" of soldiers, etc. in this play were not drilled or trained to their parts in the orthodox way. In fact, they never acted the play twice alike, but just expressed themselves as they felt at the moment. Hence the play always went with a swing — spontaneously and never mechanically. No true educational expert will need to be told that this *self-expression* is the very thing we need most to aim at in order properly to exercise and train the children's faculties and get the best results.

That the children *were* set thinking for themselves by means of playing their own version of Shakespeare's "Henry V" is proved by the fact that on the next "Unseen Reader" morning, following the first performance of "Henry V," there was a great rush for historical works of all kinds, and very shortly we heard such remarks as "Why, it was my son, Henry VI, who caused Joan of Arc's death!" (from the boy who had impersonated Henry V). "Yes, and when Jack died ("Jack" was Henry V for the nonce!) Katharine married Owen Tudor, and that's where the Tudor line came from," said another. "How do you know that?" said I. "I traced it on this table," was the reply. I looked at the book shown me. It was opened at a genealogical table! Fancy that studied voluntarily by an ordinary boy!

Then a quiet, reserved boy — Ernest, otherwise Earl of Exeter — woke up from a brown study to say, "I have found a fine piece of poetry all about it." His book was "Ballads of English History," and he looked as though he were really and thoroughly delighted. What a great improvement on the highly colored and sensational literature which is devoured by young lads so constantly! I quote this incident to illustrate that the dramatic method of teaching shows, or rather leads to, the *right way of using the textbook* as a book of reference, voluntarily approached, rather than a book the contents of which have to be committed to memory in stated doses.

And if any one should wonder whether the pupils were really able to pursue any original investigations of their own from this play, I may mention that they found out without my telling them that Henry V claimed the crown of France from his ancestor, Edward III, and learned about the Salic law. They themselves suggested that Henry VI inherited his weakness of character from his maternal grandfather, the French king whom Shakespeare painted as almost imbecile.

As time went on the children became more ambitious. They naturally desired to dive deeper into the works of a dramatist who could provide them with such keen enjoyment in playing the life of Henry V. And this is not the least significant part of the work. "We needs must love the highest *when we see it.*" We do not need to be told that each one must find and see the highest for himself. How many a poor elementary-school child is doomed never to see it! If he leaves school without having had a glimpse of it, however shadowy and distant, the chances are that he will never see it. His may be a life of toil, and his short leisure hours may be filled by the sensational "recreation" of the trick bicycle rider and other attractions of the variety theater — good or harmless in themselves perhaps, but not sufficient to take the place of the pure pleasure and elevating benefit to be derived from real enjoyment of good literature. If we can give the child a taste for good literature while still a pupil in the elementary school, we shall have opened the door by which he can, if he will, attain the highest. With a literature such as ours it is surely our duty to use such methods as will bring about this result.

And, I ask you, will a child who has once lived for a time in the romantic Forest of Arden with Touchstone, Rosalind, and Orlando ever need to be shown in what volume he may find a way of escape from a sordid world of toil and worldly gain? If he has ever taken a part in playing the delightful "A Midsummer Night's Dream," will he need to be at a loss where to find an evening's recreation? If you have ever found delight or profit or improvement in Shakespeare's pages, you will know exactly how, by association of ideas, his plays haunt one's happiest hours.

The workingman need not necessarily — because he is a workingman — blow hideous noises and rude songs on a cornet, and generally make an exhibition of himself while on his annual "outing." I do not think it is too extravagant a dream to hope that one might see such things relegated to the limbo of the past. I know young enlightened workingmen who know their English literature well; who prefer to spend all their leisure time on their bicycles, touring this country of ours; who see romance in the storied monuments of the past; who are *not* bored by an evening in the country alone or with a kindred spirit; who have the true artist's feeling for color in beautiful landscapes; who do not merely regard a patch of bright yellow mustard as so much food for sheep, but as a touch of color and contrast in the landscape; who know the names, abodes, and habits of all the flowers — rare or common —

of their countryside; who know all the wonders and all the romance of the traces of our ancestors to be found in historic sections! And that, not merely from folk legend and ignorance, but from the folk legend plus an intelligent store of knowledge obtained by reading and reasoning. Surely there is ground for encouragement when education of the right sort can turn out a workingman of this type. He will not be a less skillful or industrious worker because he is well read. A refined and intellectual workingman is often looked upon as a rarity and even with suspicion. I have hopes that the exact opposite may in time be true, and that it will be the man who works only that he may have money to spend on sensational enjoyments whom we shall call extraordinary. I have seen in my own village workingmen—including farm and garden laborers—who could not only sit through an evening of Shakespearean plays as spectators with intelligent enjoyment, but who could and did themselves give a splendid rendering of " Julius Cæsar."

That the pupils appreciated Shakespeare out of school hours was clear, for fourteen of them chose volumes of his plays for their school prizes. They further took the trouble to specify which plays they wanted included, and the favorites seemed to be "A Midsummer Night's Dream," "As You Like It," "The Merchant of Venice," "King John," "Henry V," "Julius Cæsar," and "Henry VI." These they afterwards carried backward and forward between home and school, and made themselves well acquainted with the contents in the same way that they studied " Henry V."

The girls, in particular, enjoyed the romantic plays of Shakespeare, while the boys preferred the more bustling historical plays. Their rendering of the scene between Hubert and Arthur in "King John" was quite different from any I have ever seen given by schoolboys. If any person should like an experience similar to mine, let him set a few boys to prepare and act this scene as they imagine it really took place, first reading the play carefully. I always see the boys in my mind's eye when I read the words of the play. The two attendants draped themselves in window curtains (which looked like "villains' cloaks") and wore black paper masks — pieces of paper, with holes cut for eyes, tied round their heads. They carried a pail of coals such as road repairers use at night, and had two pieces of sharp iron stuck therein. The hot coals and red-hot irons were simulated with red chalk! The boy who impersonated Hubert was, I feel sure, a born artist. Instead of reciting his lines as if he were reading them word for word, he "thought" them, and showed his thoughts in gesture and facial expression. The result was that all his young audience understood the struggle going on in "Hubert's" mind and were consequently interested, as children will be by anything which bears the stamp of truth — is "really true." The young "Arthur" of the piece, taking his cue from "Hubert," showed how the real Arthur must have gained and followed up the advantages of his eloquent and touching appeals — so much so that the audience was carried away. The same was true of the two attendants, one of whom really meant what he said when

he ejaculated, "I am best pleased to be from such a deed."
The charm of the children's presentation of these plays of
Shakespeare lay in their original treatment and interpre-
tation of them, their novel "properties" and gestures.

This brings me to mention another point — the fact
that naturally the plays in school brought forth an accompanying *handicraft* and *art* of their own. Following the
earlier plays, I frequently found the older boys drawing
in their books the scenes which they had enacted, and this
led to my giving them time and opportunity to depict
what they saw or imagined while acting or looking on.
The curious part of the resulting drawings was the fact
that they showed costume and scenery as it ought to be,
and not as seen in the make-believe plays. For instance,
in the tournament scene taken from " Ivanhoe," the boy
who drew the picture had most correctly imagined the lists
of Ashby de la Zouch, because, to him, the school desks and
cupboards had not existed in the play. He had drawn heroes
in armor instead of his small schoolmates in corduroy.

In addition to drawing, both boys and girls took a great
interest in making the various articles needed in their
plays, and I fancy this brought forth their ingenuity more,
and had a greater educational value, than formal lessons in
handicrafts — that is, for elementary-school children. It
set them experimenting at any rate, and thus they found
out their own weakness of method and ignorance of tech-
nique. It seemed, indeed, as if dramatizing lessons touched
some human interest which *must* express itself in every
possible form of art.

Photograph by Clarke and Hyde

SCHOOL GARDEN — THE FLOWER GARDENS

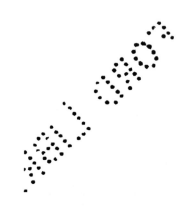

Another point which was brought out more particularly in connection with the Shakespearean plays, in which the children spoke the lines verbatim, was the habit of the small children of the chorus in arming themselves with copies of the play in progress, and constituting themselves "prompters." I have seen as many as fourteen books being closely scanned by twice as many heads of little grade children, and I have then thought, "What a splendidly attentive reading class!" What is more, I am sure they were all attentive, because, did the performers miss one single word, every child who had a book would supply the needed correction at once.

One of the most suitable and successful Shakespearean scenes for the boys was " King Henry VI," Part II, Act IV, scene ii. The boys also attempted scenes iii and iv, and scene x. Having thus exemplified the rebellion of Jack Cade, it was natural that they should read the context around it, and then dovetail what they had learned with what they had played of " King Henry V." In this way the Shakespearean play was not only valuable as a lesson in literature, but it correlated many useful branches of knowledge.

The boys liked this play so well that they modeled and played Wat Tyler's rebellion on similar lines. They commenced their play by causing two gentlemen to meet and discuss the rising in France.

SCENE I

FIRST GENTLEMAN (Squire Balderdash!) I have just heard, by a mounted messenger from Dover, that the English peasants are rising too, and are discontented with the taxes they have to pay.

SECOND GENTLEMAN. The king must be informed of this.

FIRST GENTLEMAN. But the king will not listen. He is young and hot-headed; besides, money must be raised to pay for the war with France. The peasants are headed by a man named Walter Tyler, of Essex, and they are marching to London. [*Noise of* Rabble *heard approaching. A* Crowd *gathers round a* Man, *who begins to address them with*

"When Adam delved and Eve span,
Who was then the gentleman?"]

SECOND GENTLEMAN. Come! I to the King—you to the lord mayor! Something must be done to prepare London.   [*Exeunt both quickly*]

THE PREACHER (John Ball). Brethren, I have come to explain to you the question of these illegal taxes. How can you pay them without money? (*A Voice.* We wants better wages.) Why should you poor people be oppressed, because money is needed to pay for wars? (*Another Voice.* Those who make wars should pay for 'em — we wants trade improved. We wants permission to buy and sell in the markets!) And if you are bound to pay taxes, why shouldn't you be free men and no longer serfs? (*A Voice.* Yes, that's it! We wants land to till; land at fourpence an acre.)

SCENE II. *Dartford, Kent*

Men *found working with hoes in the field. A realistic blacksmith's shop is arranged with a desk anvil at one end. The clanging of the sledge hammers is simulated by striking an ordinary hammer on an old garden fork laid on the anvil. One corner is set apart for* WAT TYLER'S *house, in which his* Daughter *sits working. A bell is heard ringing and two* Collectors *appear, calling out,* "Oyez! Oyez!" *They go to each of the* Men *to collect the poll tax, and carry a book in which they have entered the names of all persons above the age of fifteen years. They demand three groats from every one of these. The* Men *all murmur and refer the* Collectors *to* WAT TYLER, *their champion. They call at the house of* TYLER, *who declares he has no one above the age for payment. His* Daughter *appears and one of the* Collectors, *jeering, says,* "You have one, for *she* is over fifteen." WAT TYLER, *enraged, strikes him with his smith's hammer. He falls dead. The other* Collector *escapes. The* Men *rally round* TYLER *and throw the body down a well* (this is a brisk piece of acting), *and with much shouting determine to march to London. They decide on the terms they mean to demand: slavery abolished; no tolls and taxes on trade; land at fourpence per acre; better housing; no illegal taxation.*

Feeling that the schoolroom space was all too cramped for a march to freedom, the boys elected to march round the playground between the scenes and arrive in London in style. This they used to do, and frequently they introduced funny little interludes, as, for instance, meeting with a lawyer.

WAT TYLER. Ho, there! Stand! Who are you, sirrah?

LAWYER. I am a lawyer.

TYLER. Can you write?

LAWYER. Indeed, I can write a court hand.

MOB. He has been writing these heavy taxes on the poor. Away with him! [*He is dragged off, and another* Man *enters*]

TYLER. Come, sirrah, join our ranks. We march to freedom.

MAN. I am sorry, sir, I am not fit for so grand an army; besides, my wife and family need me at home.

TYLER. Can you read or write? ·

MAN. No, sir, and I am sorry for it.

TYLER. Do not be sorry. You are just the man for us. Fall in with us. [*The* Man *is pushed into a place and they march on*]

SCENE III

Arrival in London. The scene opens after the taking of London Bridge. WAT TYLER *holds a conversation with his* Chief Officer. (*Notice here how ingeniously the young playwrights make the characters tell the story in the natural course of the play. They have, no doubt, caught that unawares from Shakespeare's plays.*)

WAT TYLER. Well, what news? Did you burn the old Duke of Lancaster's palace, the Savoy?

OFFICER. Ay, marry, that did we; and right well he deserved it, spending the good money and coming home from France without accomplishing anything, but losing everything. We have lost all save Calais!

WAT TYLER. Yes, indeed! Well, I have set fire to the King's prison — the Marshalsea — and set free the prisoners. My good boys of Kent have killed every Fleming they could find, whether in church, house, or hospital. None have escaped. Now whom shall we send as messengers to the King?

OFFICER. We have here a schoolmaster who hath repented him of his learning. Shall we send him?

WAT TYLER. Bring him to me. Now, sirrah, hearken. You are to go to the King in the Tower and say, "Your Majesty, Wat Tyler hath business with ye, and requires to see ye!" Mind your manners, as becometh a messenger from a great man.

[Schoolmaster *bows low and departs. At the extreme end of schoolroom he enters the Tower gates (a gap between two desks) and is stopped by two* Warders *and asked his business. He makes low bows and persuades them to let him enter. But he has no sooner commenced his message than the young* KING (Richard II), *looking half amused, half angry, says,* "Who admitted this man? Be off, rough rebel!" *The* Messenger *returns and reports this to* WAT TYLER, *who is enraged and says,* "Go back and tell him we desire to speak with him peaceably, but if he will not meet us we shall send him messages of fire and plunder!"

[*The* Messenger *once more gets past the* Warders, *and, on his delivering his message with many awkward bows, the* KING *confers with his* Knights *and* Courtiers. *They advise him to seem to agree with* WAT TYLER *and his* Followers, *and he promises to meet the* Insurgents *on the following morning*]

SCENE IV

The Mob *under* WAT TYLER *arrive from the playground to meet the young* KING, *who, however, merely comes in a barge (inverted bench) down the River Thames to speak with them from that point of vantage. The* Mob *rush forward and attempt to reach the boat with boat hooks (map poles). There are confused shouts of* "We want no illegal taxes!" *etc., and* WAT TYLER *raises the cry of* "Treason!" *Again* WAT TYLER *sends a* Messenger, *and the* KING *promises to meet them in a field at Mile End*]

SCENE V. *Mile End*

The Mob *drawn up under* WAT TYLER *at one end of schoolroom. The* KING *and his* Followers, *mounted, at the other. (This gave an opportunity for using the horse brasses, mentioned earlier in this volume, on the king's prancing "steed.")*

KING. [*Riding forward*] I am your King and Lord, good people, what will you?

FAIRIES IN "A MIDSUMMER NIGHT'S DREAM"

WAT TYLER. Your Majesty, we will that you free us and our lands forever; that you give us leave to buy and sell in the market places; that land shall be fourpence an acre; and that no illegal taxes be levied.

MOB. Yes, yes! We want better houses. We will not be serfs any more.

KING. I grant it. Go home quietly to your houses, and I will have the charter written out and sealed.

MOB. Hurrah! Long live Richard II!

WAT TYLER. Half of you disperse to your homes. The other twenty thousand remain here with me. Captains, see to it!

SCENE VI. *Smithfield*

WAT TYLER, *mounted, talks in undertones with his* Captains. *Suddenly the* KING *and his* Followers *ride in*

WAT TYLER. [*Rides forward to meet him, and takes hold of his* "Horse's" *bridle*] You have broken your promise! Where is the charter you swore to send us?

WILLIAM WALWORTH (Mayor of London). [*Rides forward, drawing his dagger (the wooden dagger covered with silver paper in cardboard sheath mentioned before in this book*)] Take your hand from the King's rein, vile peasant. [TYLER *struggles to retain his hold of the rein. The* "Horses" *prance about.* WALWORTH *strikes* TYLER *with the dagger. He falls, groans, and dies. The* Peasants *rush forward*]

PEASANTS. They have slain our leader! Kill! kill!

KING. [*Faces round, shouting*] What need ye, my masters? I am your Captain and your King! Follow me! I will be your leader! [*He rides toward the door, facing about and waving his sword boldly. The* Mob *appear to waver for an instant, then follow him, cheering*]

The boys always finished the play by allowing "Richard" to ride out and around the playground, while they marched after him, cheering.

I think the reader will at once see clearly how Shakespeare's play and his version of Jack Cade's rebellion had influenced the young playwrights in their compilation of "Wat Tyler's Rebellion." They dragged in a "lawyer" who could write a "court hand," where Shakespeare had introduced a schoolmaster. They certainly had tried to talk in the correct style of the times. For the facts and plot they read John Richard Green's "Readings from English History" and Froissart's account of the events. The whole of the preparation and arrangement was their own, the bulk of the work falling on "Wat Tyler" himself, who also impersonated Squire Balderdash in scene i, and on his chief officer, who was also John Ball, in the same scene. The chorus, of course, informed us that the young king was only sixteen years of age, and after the play told us the results of the rising.

I can assure the reader that, under this most graphic kind of teaching, historical characters like those of Richard II and Wat Tyler are no longer vague, unreal figures with curious names, tiresome acts, and elusive dates. Certainly

they are real (and children love the concrete, we know!),
and for this reason it is impossible that any pupil should
be dull or that his brain should be inactive during such
a lesson.

The next Shakespearean play which they attempted
was the "Merchant of Venice," beginning with the trial
scene and including also scene ii, Act IV. And here I
would draw attention to the fact that there are many difficult lines, especially for "Portia," to be committed to
memory. These small rural pupils had no difficulty in
learning them *in a few days*, and after that never needed
prompting. Not that they were what is termed "sharp at
learning"; they were learning almost involuntarily, because
they were "living in the part" as it were. And that they
did not shirk learning is proved by the fact that, of his
own accord, "Shylock" in the play asked to be allowed to
act scene iii, Act I, in spite of the great number of lines
and awkwardly turned phrases it contained.

Their impersonation of the various parts, far from being
calculated to draw a smile (which might be expected when
young children attempted to act complex characters), was
earnest and interesting. "Shylock" and "Portia," on
whom so much of the success of the play depended, realized their parts, and yet played in an original manner, because the action and gesture were their own, and were
neither taught by an instructor nor copied from players
seen previously. They had merely the text of Shakespeare
to depend upon. That they read this aright was proved
by the fact that in such speeches as Shylock's, commencing

"How like a fawning publican he looks!" the boy impersonator used a venomous kind of undertone; and when Bassanio enters next and Shylock has to say, "I am debating of my present store," etc., the boy changed his tone at once to a conciliatory, cringing one, although no such directions are given in the play.

This play had, of course, no historical connection to teach, nor had "A Midsummer Night's Dream" nor "As You Like It," so we treated them as dramatized literature, under the general title of "English."

The children's playing had reached quite a finished standard by the time they attempted scenes from "A Midsummer Night's Dream." Their best scenes proved to be those of Act V, which depict "rude mechanics" in a Greek play. The school children seemed to grasp, at first reading, all Shakespeare's subtle burlesques and humors, and were eager to "dress" the piece properly. They gathered a huge quantity of ivy and wreathed the room, making archways of thin laths nailed together — here the "natural" handicraft once more made itself evident — and fastening ivy and boughs of greenery on to that foundation. Ingenuity showed itself when colored ribbons — "gold" — were needed to bind the stockings like sandals. The girls actually painted white tape with the yellow water color from their painting palettes. When dry, this answered their purposes perfectly. Afterwards, when they needed colored "ribbon" to sell by the yard while playing at arithmetic, each girl painted a piece of white tape a different color. They made Greek tunics from old cotton skirts, gathering up the waistband for a neckband, and cutting a hole at each side for the arms. These, when decorated with "key pattern" borders of gold paper (ironed on, as described before) and accompanied by long white stockings, bound like sandals, and "gold" tape fillets around the head, gave quite a picturesque and Greek appearance to the prosaic schoolroom. The girls who had long hair turned it up all round to add to the effect.

And all this was of their own initiative. Their "English" lesson was seasoned with the same fresh enthusiasm as their history lesson — with how little trouble on the part of either teacher or child! Certainly it required no more trouble or exertion in preparation than an ordinary game; yet at the end what a splendid harvest of lasting results in the wider outlook, the closer study of humanity, the enriched and strengthened memory, the greater knowledge of the beauties of our language (caught instinctively from contact with the mind of a past master in the art of appropriate clothing of expression) — and all this lasting treasure absorbed from and through a game in school! I doubt if by any other means the children could have learned to appreciate the beauties of speech such as the alliteration contained in the following lines: "The riot of the tipsy Bacchanals, tearing the Thracian singer." . . . "The thrice three Muses mourning for the death of learning," and "Whereat, with blade, with bloody blameful blade, he bravely broach'd his boiling bloody breast." These lines, which occur in "A Midsummer Night's Dream," were declaimed in a manner which brought out all their word painting ; and shortly after the play had been shown by the children to their schoolfellows the older pupils essayed to write some poetry of their own, in which we found occurring such lines as this: "Sing a song of sunshine that will suit this summer's day" — an example of alliteration which also suggested summer breezes. Again in the same poem we had, "And the leaves will fan you gently as they rustle in the breeze."

I do not think it a small matter that children should be made to understand grace of expression and a little of the way to use their own language — to avoid being tedious through using the same words over and over again from a scanty vocabulary. Only a very short time ago a member of the London County Council Education Committee was reported to have said that if a certain circular had been written in words reminiscent of the language of Milton, it would not have been understood by the people for whom it was intended. Another member described the circular as "bad grammar and bad form." A woman defended it by stating that the composition was partly her own, and that its style had been adopted as "being more likely to interest the people." If such conditions prevail among the masses, then it is high time that Shakespeare and his English became "familiar in their mouths as household words." Surely the best grammar or composition lessons must be long drafts from the well of pure English to be found in our standard authors. Somehow we have always felt this more or less vaguely, and have tried bringing our horses to the well; but they did not always drink, and seldom deeply.

I wonder whether we grown-ups would ever have been so fond of Shakespeare's plays if we had merely read them, especially if we had been ordered to read them! Do we not remember how and when our real, lively interest was awakened? In how many cases was it the illuminating acting and impressive delivery of some great Shakespearean actor that first roused our interest? Perhaps afterwards we read the play over again quietly, and by association of ideas felt the same pleasurable sensations. Perhaps, also, it will not be a national waste of time if our masses learn to love Shakespeare " in the days of their youth " by such means as I have described earlier in the chapter. It means to the masses exactly what it means to the few — an enriched vocabulary, a better-stocked mind, a more fertile imagination; for the days when people talked in the language of Shakespeare and his compeers, and consequently *thought* in that language, were the days of vivid imagination, initiative, and adventure. Our empire was extended by discovery; our trade was improved by intelligence; our inventions were made to keep pace with the demand for greater luxury, which was the outcome of refinement of thought — refined, that is, in comparison with pre-Elizabethan times.

It may seem a sweeping statement, but is it not true that, in spite of at least more than twenty years of compulsory teaching of English, written and oral, the average youth confines himself to the latest catchword to express everything ? One feels that he cannot forgive an English-speaking person for neglecting the beauties of his own language — a language in which almost every word tells a history; in which is written a literature unrivaled in the world. And the only way to revive the use of correct English is to allow children in school to speak and read it almost constantly. My own experience is, that allowing them to act a part saves them from feeling conscious of speaking or reading as a *lesson*, and causes them to use the words with a sense of their æsthetic beauty.

My pupils involuntarily bore me out in this opinion, for they asked whether they might read a play, and, taking the various parts, chose for their first effort "As You Like It." They liked it so well that for quite a number of weeks it was always asked for on Friday afternoons, which afternoon we always set apart for sports or any subject that seemed to please the largest number. The Celia and Rosalind of the play were good friends, and, as most of the actors had their own copies of the piece, it was evident that these two studied their parts together at home during the evenings. They all soon became quite expert at reading and acting at the same time, and I feel sure that this improved their reading immensely. We seldom heard a word mispronounced. On the contrary, we heard great improvement in tone of voice, inflection, and modulation.

It may seem incredible, but I am certain that even the younger pupils thoroughly enjoyed and appreciated the play when they saw it acted by their schoolfellows. Of course the actors put their own original little stamps upon it. Once more they improvised costumes, using their fingers with much ingenuity. "Audrey" was attired in an old ragged "window-curtain" skirt, with her brother's boots, many sizes too big, until on one joyful day a small boy proudly marched into school bearing a pair of real wooden shoes, in which "Audrey" clumped about to her heart's content. "Orlando," not to be behindhand, used to hang his verses on the school palm, which was always placed in the center of the "stage" to represent the Forest of Arden. "Touchstone" wore a red flannel cap and bells, homemade of course, and "Corin" had a real shepherd's crook, borrowed from his father.

By this time the reader will have realized that I did not attempt to teach stagecraft, but that my aim was rather to put this in the background; yet our child "Rosalind," our "Celia," and our "Puck" were so exceedingly good, dramatic, and convincing in their parts that their performance really approached pure art. A great Shakespearean actor and actress who saw them waxed quite enthusiastic over their natural way of conducting themselves, and compared it with the "trained trickery" of many actors who are taught to "raise the hand here, walk so many strides there, lower the voice so, speak more slowly," and so forth.

After all, "all the world's a stage." What were all our heroes of history but men who held the center of the world's stage for a time, and so acted their daily parts that they made a success of their play ? What is our own every-day demeanor but the part which we play to express our-selves, or the reverse, according as our humor dictates ? So that, left to themselves, our small pupils had only to imagine themselves the characters they represented, and they immediately comported themselves as they fancied those characters would have in the circumstances shown in the play.

I have mentioned the arches of greenery used for " A Midsummer Night's Dream." These were used again for the Forest of Arden when the play was carried out in school ; but whenever possible we had the play in the open air, on the downs or under the trees in the playground.

CHAPTER VI

A GIRLS' PLAY .

THE girls were so pleased with their own successful readings of "As You Like It," that they determined to write a play, as the boys had done, entirely by themselves, each character making her own speeches from whatever authority she could collect material. They chose scenes from the closing part of the life of Mary Queen of Scots, and I will copy one of the girls' manuscripts exactly as it was made.

EXECUTION OF MARY QUEEN OF SCOTS

SCENE I

Enter QUEEN MARY *and* Ladies in Waiting. *The* QUEEN *seats herself at a table and the* Ladies *sit grouped at needlework. A knock is heard*

QUEEN MARY. Go and see who that is knocking at the door.

ELIZABETH (Lady in Waiting). Yes, your Majesty. [*She goes to the door and talks in an undertone to some one outside, then returns*] It is Lord Shrewsbury, and he requires to see you, your Majesty.

QUEEN MARY. Tell him I cannot see him just at present.

ELIZABETH. [*Goes back to door and speaks to messenger*] My lady says she cannot see you just at present.

SHREWSBURY. But tell her my business is very important, and therefore I *must* see her.

ELIZABETH. [*Returning*] Madam, he says his business is very important, so therefore he must see you.

QUEEN MARY. [*After musing for a while*] Well, then, tell him I will see him.

Enter SHREWSBURY

SHREWSBURY. I am very sorry to tell you, madam, that you are condemned to death. To-morrow at eight o'clock you are to die. Therefore prepare yourself, madam.

QUEEN MARY. [*Half fainting, speaks to the* Ladies *who run and support her*] What does he say?

SHREWSBURY. I am very sorry to tell you, madam, that you are condemned to death. To-morrow at eight o'clock you are to die. Therefore prepare yourself, madam.

QUEEN MARY. Can it be true that the Queen of England has consented to my death?

SHREWSBURY. It is true, madam. [*He shows the warrant*] See, there is her signature!

QUEEN MARY. I solemnly protest, with my hand on this Testament [*laying her hand on volume on the table*], that I have never done anything that could prejudice the welfare of the kingdom.

[*Exit* SHREWSBURY *after bowing low*]

QUEEN MARY. [*Rising*] Come, my ladies, supper — the last, alas! — awaits us. Do not weep for me!

ELLEN AND MALCOLM GRAEME

JEAN (Lady in Waiting). Oh, my lady, we would do anything if only we could see you happy.

[*Exit* QUEEN *slowly; the* Ladies *follow her, weeping*]

SCENE II

QUEEN MARY *seated at a table.* Ladies *as before*

QUEEN MARY. Go and fetch me my handkerchiefs.

ELIZABETH. Yes, your Majesty. [*She brings them in a box. The* QUEEN *turns them over and at last holds up one*]

QUEEN MARY. I will have this one with the gold border to bandage my eyes on the scaffold to-morrow.

[Ladies *sob aloud*]

QUEEN MARY. [*Pointing to each one of her* Ladies *in turn as they sit around her*] To you, Jean, I leave all my rings; to you, Elizabeth, my jewels; to you my dresses; to you my ponies; and to you my money. Ask Bourgoin, my physician, to attend and read my will.

Enter BOURGOIN *with the will*

BOURGOIN. I here bequeath all my jewels, dresses, rings, ponies, money, and other things to my ladies in waiting. [*He turns to the* QUEEN] Will you sign it, madam? [*The* QUEEN *dips a quill pen in the ink, and after pausing a moment signs it. The* Ladies *all cover their eyes with their handkerchiefs*]

BOURGOIN. You will need two witnesses, madam.

QUEEN MARY. Elizabeth and Jean, you will sign this, please. [*Both* Ladies *come up weeping and sign it*]

JEAN. [*Falling on her knees in front of the* QUEEN] Oh, madam, we would willingly give our lives if only we could see you happy once more.

[*Exit* BOURGOIN *after bowing. The* QUEEN *then rises and goes off, her Ladies following her*]

SCENE III

QUEEN MARY, *kneeling as if in prayer. A knocking is heard at the door and a bell strikes eight o'clock*

QUEEN MARY. Tell those intruders to wait a little.

JEAN. Yes, madam. [*The* Sheriff, *bearing a white wand, pushes past her, and enters*]

SHERIFF. Madam, the lords await you, and have sent me to you. Are you ready?

QUEEN MARY. Yes, quite ready. Let us go.

[*She rises from her knees. She walks with difficulty, so two of her Ladies support her. At the end of the room she is met by the* EARLS OF SHREWSBURY *and* KENT. *The* EARL OF SHREWSBURY *orders the* Ladies *in* Waiting *to stand back. They refuse.* JEAN *exclaims,* "No, never!" *They cling to her dress and finally fall on their knees. When they have succeeded in removing the* Ladies, *the* QUEEN *walks on a few steps, with dignity. She then meets* ANDREW MELVIL, *her trusty serva t. He falls on his knees, weeping*]

QUEEN MARY. Thank you, good Melvil, for your constant fidelity. Tell my son all that you know and all that you are about to witness.

MELVIL. It will be the most sorrowful message I ever carried, to announce to the world that my sovereign and dear mistress is dead.

QUEEN MARY. Thou shouldst rather rejoice, good Melvil, that Mary Stuart has arrived at the close of her misfortunes. Bear these tidings, that I die a true Scotchwoman, a true Frenchwoman. Thou knowest that this world is only vanity, and full of troubles and misery. May God forgive those who have sought my death. The Judge of the secret thoughts and actions of men knows that I have always desired the union of Scotland and England. Commend me to my son, and tell him that I have never done anything that could prejudice the welfare of the kingdom, or his quality as king, or detract in any respect from our sovereign prerogative.

KENT. [*Reads the sentence aloud slowly*] You have been found guilty of conspiring against the life of our sovereign lady Queen Elizabeth, and against her realm; therefore the sentence passed upon you is that your head shall be severed from your body.

QUEEN MARY. I am a queen born, not subject to the laws. I have never sought the life of my cousin Elizabeth.

KENT. [*Looking at the crucifix in the* QUEEN'S *hand*] It would be much better advised of you to have Christ in your heart, and not in your hand, Madam.

QUEEN MARY. I cannot hold such an object in my hand without my heart being attached to the sufferings it represents. [*The two* Executioners *approach and attempt to remove her veil, but the* QUEEN *motions them away*]

I have never had such rough valets before! Elizabeth and Jean, I require you. [*With their help she removes her veil and outer dress*] I am not accustomed to do this before so many people. [*Her* Maids *sob aloud*] Instead of weeping, you should rejoice. I am very happy to leave this world in so good a cause. [*She turns to the other* Maids] I give you all my blessing.

EXECUTIONER. [*Kneeling*] We ask your pardon, madam, for the deed we are about to do.

QUEEN MARY. I forgive you, and all the authors of my death. [JEAN *then bandages her eyes with the gold-fringed handkerchief, and all her* Maids *withdraw to the edge of the scaffold, weeping. She turns towards the block and kneels before it*] My God, I have hoped in you. I commit myself to your hands.

EXECUTIONER. God save Queen Elizabeth!

SHREWSBURY. And so perish all her enemies!

KENT. Amen!

The girls, as before, made the necessary dresses and properties, and in order to get these correct as to period and fashion, read all the available literature on the subject. Because Mary had declared herself to be a " good French-woman," they utilized a skirt embroidered with fleurs-de-lis. They copied her peculiar headdress carefully, using an old bonnet shape for the purpose and edging it with pearl beads.

I think the reader will agree that this was a very full and successful attempt to put together a play to illustrate the period. Moreover, it was an excellent writing and composition lesson, with plenty of transcription from various books to give practice in the spelling of new or difficult words, and to help form the habit of reading for reference and information. I may also add that the manuscript from which I took the foregoing play was written out from memory, the girl who wrote it having lost her first copy.

CHAPTER VII

LITERATURE

OF course the children could not lay claim to a very extensive acquaintance with English literature if they limited their dramatic readings to Shakespeare's plays or Scott's historical novels. Their field of operations was much wider, but their methods of working were still original. They learned to recite such poems as " Charge of the Light Brigade," " Ye Mariners of England," and " Death of Nelson," and introduced them into their plays — the last two into their play " Nelson," and the former into "The Crimea." They selected a boy to recite while the dead Nelson lay in state; and he certainly made us all see mental pictures. I have heard the school ask for a fourth and fifth repetition of the " Charge of the Light Brigade," that much-hackneyed school recitation! It was not hackneyed to them, of course; and they always concluded the piece by having the " Roll Call " of supposed survivors, and introduced a realistic touch by letting the last man stagger up just as his number was called, answer his name, and fall dead. It is just these little touches that children will add if they are allowed, and which make all the difference between the prosaic "memory-work" repetitions and the glorious, *real, living recitations.*

The girls, too, in this matter were very original in their own way. In June, for instance, they would organize a sort of "Rose" play. On the day on which it took place the room was tastefully decorated with roses of every sort. The older girls selected a Rose Queen and called themselves Rose maidens. Then (and here my point comes in) they found out at least one good poem or part of a poem, or passage of poetical prose, from good standard authors, and either sang or recited in turn before the "Queen," — generally accompanied by soft music on the piano, — choosing good classical compositions where possible. In this way they "discovered" some charming old poems which are not, as a rule, found in schools; for example, "The Rose had been washed, just washed in a Shower, which Mary to Anna conveyed," and "The Rose upon my Balcony." Of course they included "The Solitary Rose" and any references to roses to be found in Tennyson, Wordsworth, Shakespeare, etc., finishing with "The Last Rose of Summer" and the singing of a Sussex folk song, "Rosebuds in June."

Children would often glorify their favorite poems in a way of their own. One little girl invited a chorus of girls to help her, and trained them to act in dumb show while she recited Wordsworth's "Daffodils" in a most inspired manner, to the accompaniment of soft music, generally Mendelssohn's "Spring Song." The chorus would pretend to be daffodils, dressed in yellow and green crinkled paper; and they swayed, or danced, or nodded their heads, or went to sleep, or flashed, as the poem directed. All this was prepared and played directly after the afternoon session — for many of the older pupils would beg to be allowed to "stay in" after school hours and make up their plays and invent new ones.

Of course they very soon discovered possibilities in the works of Dickens. It had long been our rule to read the "Christmas Carol" and other Christmas tales every year just before Christmastide. Naturally when we commenced "playing" our lessons, the "Christmas Carol" showed its adaptability. The older boys and girls commenced by acting the "Cratchitts' Christmas Dinner," and used to enter most whole-heartedly into the spirit of the thing. They were able to dress the piece more easily than their historical plays, because the period represented was more modern. Bob Cratchitt wore a long white scarf, which dangled below his waistcoat. He wore the black-tailed coat which did duty for an officer's coat in the "Nelson" play. They used to draw a table up in front of the school fire on dull, dreary, wet winter afternoons, and revel in the spirit of good humor and loving kindness which Dickens designed to inculcate.

I am quite sure that in the years to come, when lessons on vulgar fractions have been long forgotten and "cob-webbed o'er," those afternoons and the lessons they taught will stand out in relief from the pages of memory.

If Shakespeare was good for their improvement in English, so Dickens was their textbook for homely good-ness. We who read and love Dickens know how magically he constructs an "atmosphere" for us — how, like a silver

MR. SCROOGE AND THE BENEVOLENT GENTLEMEN

thread running through a string of pearls, goodness and virtue connect all the emotions he stirs in us. So it was with my younger pupils. They acted the " Christmas Carol " every Christmas in their simple fashion, and all felt better for it. From Tiny Tim they learned to sympathize with all weak, afflicted things. They learned contentment and resignation from Bob Cratchitt, who earned but " fifteen of his own namesakes every week, yet the spirit of Christmas present blessed him." They learned cheerfulness and good-will from Scrooge's nephew Fred, who, although " Christmas had never put a scrap of gold or silver in his pocket," said "God bless it," and would keep his Christmas humor to the last. Even Scrooge himself had lessons to teach them — to abhor meanness and selfishness ; to be merciful ; to use Christmas as a time for putting away all grudges and quarrels, as well as for settling up all debts ; above all, not to be afraid of reforming thoroughly, when necessary, regardless of the sneers or jeers of others. Fezziwig, too, bless his heart ! who could "wink with his calves " in the good old Sir Roger de Coverley dance and " never stagger," who danced with twenty pairs of partners — "people who *would* dance, too." Will the children ever recall these school years at Christmas time without a smile and a tear for the " Fezziwigs' Ball," which they played so " really and truly" in the days gone by ? The name Fezziwig will bring back to them the fat, rosy boy (stuffed in the region of the waistcoat with dusters to complete the illusion !) who sat up at the spindle-legged desk, once the hermit's cell for Friar Tuck, and beamed over spectacles, which sat with difficulty on his snub little nose, while he called, " Hello, Dick ! Chirrup, Ebenezer ! " and we all settled down to enjoy such a good time.

It was all *real*. Truly the page was no " dead letter," but living spirit to us. How infectious was the motherly, beaming smile of Mrs. Fezziwig, bedight in cap and ribbons, and how really sorry we all felt for " the girl who had her ears boxed by her mistress," and " the boy who was suspected of not having enough to eat." I feel convinced that the mere act of playing and enjoying the " Christmas Carol " was a true education to my pupils — it drew out the latent sympathies in which they were not naturally lacking.

And I am quite sure that the type of so-called education which contents itself with such present " results " as a piece of composition, immaculately penned and all correctly spelled, while it may exhibit a glaring paucity of ideas, or is satisfied if it can show " four sums right and neatly worked," is a very poor pretense at educating worthy men and women for the battle of life. Perhaps a critic may say that the religious and moral side of the children is attended to during the daily hour for religious instruction. But if religion be not the guiding principle of our daily life, for *all* day, it becomes worse than nothing to us. It is impossible to shut away moral teaching into a compartment of the mind. It should be freely and openly diffused throughout the thoughts, to " leaven the whole lump."

Nature study, properly treated, can touch both senses and emotions — can awaken an instinct leading up to nature's God. There was a Great Teacher once who scorned not to teach the highest and grandest truths through simple parables on nature — who taught them graphically, in the open air, from observation of the actual objects. So, too, good literature can stir human emotions and guide and school human passions — can prevent us from excess of introspection, from dwelling on self; and there is more need for inculcating this love of nature and good literature in the mind of the workingman's child than in that of the child of higher station. In the latter case, the child may properly be left to parents who, if they possess education and culture, can look after the reading and moral training of their own child. But parents of the working class have no time, even if they have the ability, to direct their children's reading.

Therefore I judged it to be of vital importance that every one of my pupils should be given opportunity for getting on good terms with our English authors. We did not scorn the lighter vein, when it presented itself in the form of " The Pickwick Papers." I remember one real, all-round " dunce " being reformed and becoming a comparatively bright boy through being cast for the part of Mr. Winkle in scenes which the boys got up from the early chapters of that book. It was quite a revelation to us all to view the awakening, or rather the transformation. The fact was that, rather than look ridiculous in the eyes of his schoolfellows, he made a great effort to read and master his " part," and, in doing so, discovered his own powers, which from that time he cultivated and improved. When leaving school he expressed a desire to possess a copy of " The Pickwick Papers." He evidently did not intend throwing aside his books, but *had made a beginning and meant to go on.*

The girls were particularly fond of Louisa M. Alcott's " Little Women " — as, indeed, what girls are not ? They acted as much of this book as was possible, becoming so familiar with its contents that they could quote many of the chapters by heart. A kind friend presented us with copies of " Wood Magic " and " Bevis," both by Richard Jefferies. These three books were, I feel sure, stories of the authors' own childhood. They were tales of human children, and they appealed, therefore, to human children. The objection is often made by teachers of girls, when discussing ways and means of using the dramatic method in school, that the difficulty is that there are only girls and no boys for male parts. Meg, Jo, Beth, and Amy easily solved the difficulty, and in the story of their girlhood one can find ample material for a start. After that, you may trust the girls to be resourceful enough to find their own ways and means.

In the story of " Bevis " we have an account of how two schoolboys "played" school ; how they played a Roman battle ; how they manufactured a gun, a raft, a boat, and went on a voyage of discovery round a small lake, finding a real island and living on it ; which may all sound commonplace enough as I have described it, but

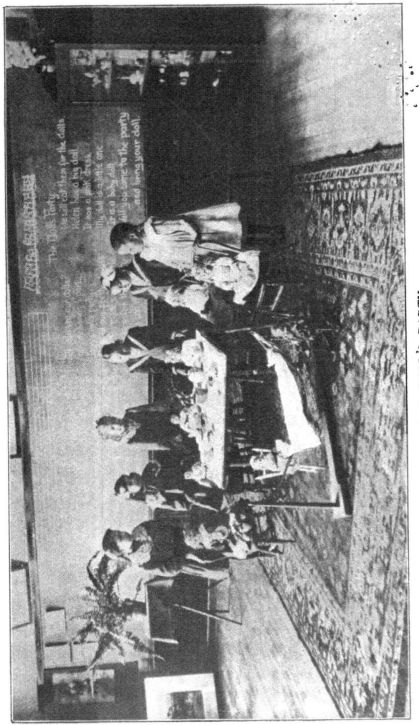

THE DOLL'S PARTY

which is very far from commonplace as written by the pen
of Jefferies in real "boy" language. Our boys, on reading it, were instantly fired with the desire to play it. I
must confess, that I was also! Bevis's first craft was an
old wooden packing case, and his scene of operations a
brook near his house. Very good packing cases we had
in plenty in the school shed, and a brook within ten minutes of the schoolhouse. The packing cases were heavy,
and July days are often hot, but down to the brook we
hied us on the hottest day I have ever experienced. The
air quivered with heat, and not the slightest particle of
shade could we find — not even a hawthorn bush. But
the spirit of adventure was upon us and would not be
quenched. A network of brooks and drains separates
our town from the seashore. These are spanned at intervals by rough wooden bridges for cattle to cross from one
pasture to the other. Bridges have always a fascination
for children, and we speedily chose the neighborhood of
one of them for our base of operations. Naturally we had
to experiment a good deal before the packing case behaved
itself properly as a raft; but when it did, and the first
passenger gently punted under the bridge, excitement ran
high. Soon off came boots and stockings, and we were in
the thick of a game. The raft went on voyages to all
kinds of places and the chorus sat along the banks to explain matters. One boy found his toes sinking into yellow
clay. "Oh, this is gold!" shouted he. "Then it must
be Africa," cried one of the chorus. "Where I have been
it is blue clay," said another. "Oh, that's diamonds!"

quickly decided the chorus; "it is South Africa." The high temperature supplied a realistic touch to the idea of "Afric's sunny fountains," and soon a "South African" game was in full progress, some of the little bare-legged boys forming an "ostrich farm."

There was no lack of interest next morning when we brought out the large map and the geography lesson began. The mere mention of South Africa brought the knowing little twinkles (which practised teachers recognize as their most encouraging sign) into all those suddenly alert eyes; tongues were loosened and every point of fact regarding that country was referred to the spot by the brooks where we had played. New names and the new facts regarding them were treasured up for naming special places by the brookside, for we had hidden our packing-case rafts in long reeds for future use. I can assure my readers that the one book, "Bevis," had led to more than passing acquaintance with good literature, for the book rendered aid to the game, and, inversely, the game lent a halo to the book.

There was another book which became immensely popular with the children. It is called "Days before History," and describes the life of a boy in prehistoric times. This book provided games which lasted for months and filled all the boys' playtimes and leisure hours. It appealed the more forcibly to children because it dealt with the life of a boy more particularly than with "grown ups." The boy was named "Tig," and to this day the children remember their "Tig" games. They even built a shed, very roughly it is true, in the lane outside the school and named it the "Tig shed." The wood was obtained from the remains of an old disused gallery and its accompany-ing desks. The boys supplied their own tools. At first they had made a hut on the hillside in the real fashion of Tig's relatives, by pulling down the lower branches of a convenient tree and pegging them to the ground, calling it their "rooftree." But they wanted to be near the school premises; so, utilizing the neighboring trees as much as possible, they built a shed, where they played at prehistoric times. They read in their "Days before History" how the first cups and other utensils were made. So after a long and diligent hunt they found a spot where the right sort of clay was to be found, and set to work according to the directions in the book. I need not tell how delighted they were to mix and knead the clay with water, using their hands, nor of the delightful mess they made on the school floor in the region of the fireplace. They proved by painful experience that prehistoric man had evidently nothing to learn from educated folks on the subject of pottery making without tools, for their first rough basins cracked in the baking process, which took place in the hot ashes piled over them. A second attempt resulted in better-shaped cups, which would stand straight and hold water. There was a great ceremony of drinking water from *the* cup. Subsequently it was placed in the school museum and often passed for a bit of real antique work.

There is very little difference between this game of making prehistoric pottery and clay-modeling lessons in school. But that bit of difference makes all the difference in the world. It is a game, not a lesson. It is enthusiastic (not to say impulsive!), not dull. It is voluntary, not forced. It teaches self-reliance, not reliance on a teacher's initiative. It is informal, not formal.

After we had played at being Stone Age folk, one can imagine that more than a casual and passing interest attached itself to some really good specimens of Stone Age ax heads, flint scrapers, and arrowheads, which had for some years reposed in the school museum. We realized how much men had lost by civilization when we tried, fruitlessly, to chip a flint into an ax head — or into any shape at all — much less to polish or grind it!

Our attempts at prehistoric cookery met with greater success. Having read directions from the history of Tig, one of the boys smuggled a herring into school, while some one else brought clay. The herring in its clay covering was placed in hot ashes under the fireplace and allowed to remain there during drawing-lesson time. A few potatoes, dug from the boys' own school garden, kept it company; but this was an anachronism, since we all knew that potatoes did not grow in England when Tig was a boy. At playtime the herring was sampled, and, of course, voted the best ever tasted — albeit the side nearest the fire was charred. An unlucky visitor who chanced to call was forced to taste the herring, and, being a man who had roughed it in Australia, he did so with very good grace indeed.

CHAPTER VIII

GEOGRAPHY

THE geography lesson gave us no trouble to dramatize and was particularly well adapted for being played as a game. The geography game began by being played in the desks with sand-modeling trays, and drawing in colors. Children would model a county or part of a country and cut out paper lighthouses, make paper boats and bridges or paper animals, and place them standing upright in the sand. Then, in turn, they would talk about them with their teacher. Again they would make colored drawings (of their own — each child originating according to his own mental impressions) to illustrate the lessons on towns or districts which had been given to them. For instance, one child, to illustrate a lesson on Reading, had drawn a large factory with horses and wagons outside. This, he explained, was a biscuit factory. Another large building appeared at the end of a roadway represented by two wavy lines. This he had labeled a jail — and so on.

Our next step in the direction of geography games was suggested by a little Grade III pupil. I discovered her one wet dinner hour with the map of the world spread out on the floor and a ring of small, eager children kneeling around it. She had a little black doll in a tiny toy boat on wheels, and she was pretending to bring it on a voyage from South Africa to England. All the while she kept up a string of sentences in squeaky broken English, supposed to be spoken by the doll.

Incidentally and unconsciously she was giving her small audience a splendid idea of the various interesting things and places passed, and even climatic conditions; for she made the doll shiver when he got into colder latitudes. Funniest of all, when she landed him at the London Docks, she produced a little tin toy railway train (ever so many sizes smaller than the doll!) and, seating him on it, rattled him off to a " woolen " town to buy a cloth overcoat. Quickly some one suggested: " Can we play it again to-morrow and then I 'll bring a little overcoat? I 'll make it to-night." Another followed with: " I 'll make him a whole suit." They were as good as their word, and on the following morning the whole class joined in the game with great gusto. The little doll was rattled all over the map of England and bought presents at every stopping place. Afterwards, of course, he was treated to a voyage home, by a different route from that taken when traveling to England. He had to show his friends his presents and tell where he bought them. Notice how, unconsciously, the children made use of repetition to strengthen memory. They were really repeating the manufactures of English towns — only they did not do it in the bad old " learning-strings-of-facts " way.

We played this and other doll games until we quite naturally drifted into substituting real live pupils for the dolls, and, once more hanging up the maps, pretended that various parts of the schoolroom, or playground, or neighborhood were the physical features of other places. This I called the geography game proper, and it originated in the classroom set apart for Grades I and II. Their first game dealt with the zones. They pretended that the north side of their room was the north pole — it happened to be the coldest side of the room, and the fireplace, being on the south side, made a very appropriate warmth for the "equator." The "arctic region" was inhabited by boys who pretended to be Esquimaux, Polar bears, seals, walruses, or reindeer. Other children pretended to be icebergs, Jack Frost, frozen sea, etc. A bright boy and girl were picked out and allowed to be travelers in the Arctic region, where they held conversations with the Esquimaux, during which the latter described the conditions under which they were supposed to live — climate, seasons, etc. The next day they varied the game by getting into a big ship — the ever-useful soap box on wheels — and being jammed in the ice floes.

Their method of representing icebergs was novel, being merely two rows of little girls with their white pinafores over their heads. They were quite glad to be anything, so long as they were "in the game," and busied themselves by making up a long speech about the iceberg, finishing with an original verse in which, I remember, "ice and snow" rimed conveniently with "Esquimaux." The Esquimau boys had a little scene of their own, pretending to break holes in the ice and spear seals and fish, the two latter being impersonated by small boys who "swam" under the desks, the tops of which represented ice. The inkwell holes were the breathing holes for the "seals."

On the third day the "iceberg" was allowed to break away from its surrounding ice under the more genial air of spring and travel to Newfoundland. En route it collided with a "ship," which it wrecked. Of course the "wreck" was the outcome of the "fog" which sprang into being on the approach of the iceberg to the shores of Newfoundland. The "fog" was composed of little girls waving their pinafores up and down. Then Newfoundland fishermen bravely came to the rescue of the wrecked Englishmen and rowed them ashore in a boat. The little girls who had been a fog now most obligingly became "codfish drying in the sun." This time the ever-versatile pinafores were dangled over backs, and their owners stood in a row with their faces to the wall. Of course the rescued men, while being accommodated in the fishermen's hut, asked questions about all that they saw. First they noticed the "codfish drying in the sun," and the fishermen told them that they caught about "one hundred and fifty millions of codfish in one year." The game then went on in a kind of dialogue:

TRAVELER. Are cod the only fish you catch?

FISHERMAN. Oh, no! We catch plenty of salmon in the rivers, too.

TRAVELER. Do the fogs trouble you on the island?

FISHERMAN. The fogs do not come any nearer than the Grand Banks out there, unless a southeast wind blows.

TRAVELER. Do you grow pretty much the same crops as we do in England?

FISHERMAN. Well, barley and oats grow everywhere, but not wheat. We have a very even and moist climate, so we grow grasses regularly.

TRAVELER. How large is this island?

FISHERMAN. Some say it is much larger than Ireland, and it is the nearest American land to Ireland.

TRAVELER. I daresay you are proud to belong to the Dominion of Canada?

FISHERMAN. [*Indignantly*] That is just where you Englishmen show ignorance. We do not belong to Canada. We are a separate colony — Britain's oldest colony!

TRAVELER. Oh, I am sorry I made such a mistake, but I shall make no mistake if I say what a splendid harbor you have here.

FISHERMAN. Ah! you may say that with truth. The harbor of St. John's is one of the very best on the Atlantic coast. [*Here the rest of the* Class *stamp loudly on the floor*]

TRAVELER. What is that?

FISHERMAN. That's the thirty-two pounder. It will go off every half hour in foggy weather. [Class *make prolonged siren hoot*] And that's a compressed air trumpet which blows every minute to warn ships.

The reader can, no doubt, trace the influence of the textbook on geography in this dialogue. The point is, that the dry matter is broken up into dialogue, and, by means of action, movement, interest, and repetition is rendered easy to memorize.

Naturally, the first game being a success, another was soon in progress, and this time the travelers set out for the warm end of the room, otherwise the equator and the torrid zone. This time also a boy represented the Emperor Equator, and the torrid zone was his sun palace. Children impersonated elephants, tigers, and serpents. The travelers were supposed to be bitten by the latter and to fall ill, etc. They found large butterflies and mosquitoes. One of them caught the fever. One part of the room became a jungle, very hot, with no rain for a long time, and then suddenly torrents of rain (imitated by children tapping one finger on the palm of the other hand like the pattering of rain). The travelers got into swampy ground, where they found the hippopotamus rolling in the muddy pools, and the rhinoceros. Of course the boys thoroughly enjoyed representing these animals. It was also quite to their taste to be native bearers. They rigged up two bamboo poles with sacking stretched across them and gave the travelers rides across the swampy ground in fine style. During the whole time dialogue was kept up and the various "animals" acted their parts — the travelers asking questions in the style of the previous game and the natives answering them. Crossing the rivers the travelers had hairbreadth escapes from crocodiles and alligators. Now and again they stalked and shot an antelope, and a boy with a long neck was selected for a giraffe. The school palm was supposed to be a date palm. Some one brought real dates, which the travelers pretended to gather and eat. As each child was expected to represent some person or thing if possible, they were sometimes puzzled to find something which had not already been chosen by a companion ; and to show how well they looked up their subject, they chose, in addition to the things already mentioned, aloes, coffee, gold and gold dust, gorillas, chimpanzees, parrots, and ostriches.

The other zones furnished games of a similar sort with, of course, the little variations and originalities which children will introduce into the games they play spontaneously.

Grade III next essayed the geography game, and (here comes in the benefit to be derived from allowing the scholars to make their personality felt in the choice of means of expression) their game had more of real play in it than of drama. Their first game they styled '' Coal and Iron Towns.'' From their geography books they picked out the names of all the towns in England specially noted for coal or iron produce. These they printed with colored paints on drawing paper, in type large enough to be read by all the children in the class at once when held in front of their desks. The name of the town was printed very large, and underneath appeared the names of the articles for which the town was noted. This occupied but a very short time when each child undertook one ticket. Then they chose boys or girls to hold the tickets in front of the class, having first placed them in positions as nearly as possible approaching the correct geographical locations on the map. The director of the game appointed himself a merchant in an office, with a telephone and a type-writer. The telephone, by the way, was a long string with a tin lid fastened at each end. He waited until the whole class had been given time to master fairly well the names of the towns and their produce. Then all the "towns" turned their tickets blank side outwards. The "merchant" telephoned to the "office" (otherwise the class) to "send up Mr. So-and-so," naming one of the boys. Mr. So-and-so duly came up and received his orders. Perhaps they were: "Mr. So-and-so, you are to go to all the 'iron' towns of England and bring me samples of iron from each. I have written to the principal firms and told them that you will call for samples."

Mr. So-and-so then had to board a train (a boy's back, of course!), which stopped at *every* town. If it were an "iron" town, he was to get out, get a sample of iron, and go on again. If it were not, he must sit still in the train until it moved off again.

The train would start amid much screeching, whistling, and steam-engine noises. Pulling up at the first "station," which would perhaps be Newcastle-on-Tyne, the boy hold-ing the name card would call out "Newcastle! New-castle!" Should Mr. So-and-so sit still and impassive, the train would presently move on again; but should he, from ignorance, alight from the train and demand, "A sample of your iron, please," the holder of the name card would triumphantly turn it round and show "noted for coal, ship-building, machinery, chemicals, glass." A telephone mes-sage would be flashed along to the master: "Your man

GEOGRAPHY GAMES—"COAL AND IRON TOWNS"

wasting his time at Newcastle." Should he pass an "iron" town and fail to alight, a telephone message would be sent: "Your man neglected to call at Middlesbrough."

The "master" made a note of all these little messages, and when his "man" came to report himself and show his samples, his errors would be pointed out to him and a certain sum docked from his wages. He was sometimes told that his services as traveler would not be required again. The fun of the game came next; for, as the "man" returned from the "master's" office, the "towns" drew up in two rows facing each other, and he had to "run the gauntlet" to the tune of "Newcastle for coal; Middlesbrough for iron," to the accompaniment of playful blows with handkerchiefs. The game would progress until all the chorus had taken their turn at being traveler.

The class next made out tickets for a game combining "cotton and woolen" towns of England, and played it in a similar way, afterwards making up another game including all the other manufactures which they could find out about. As soon as the manufactures were so well known that the chorus made very few, if any, mistakes, the class attempted more dramatic geography.

They would take one county or district and try to represent it in the form of a play. They followed the order of their textbook on geography and began with the northern counties, and not, as one might have supposed, with Sussex or London. Their dramatic rendering of Cumberland and the Lake District was interesting and amusing. The chorus of little girls before referred to in this chapter knelt on the floor, forming an irregular oval as nearly like the shape of Lake Windermere as the space would permit. Each one of them then delivered a speech about the lake. On the whole, the speeches were fairly correct and had the merit of being original. Here is one :

" We are the lake fairies. We live on Lake Winder. mere. It is a beautiful lake of clear water studded with islands. It is the longest, largest, and most beautiful lake in the district, and I am sure it well deserves the name of ' Queen of the Lakes.' It is fourteen miles in length, and in one place it is forty fathoms deep. Look there towards the north and see how it is surrounded by grand peaks and mountain masses. Perhaps you can see the ' mighty Helvellyn.' From its southern end it sends out the River Leven, which runs into Morecambe Bay."

A party of the older pupils of the class now pretended to be Lancashire people out on an excursion to the Lake District. They arranged a railway station at each end of the room, and a train (two soap boxes — one for engine and one for carriages !); then, after buying tickets, with cardboard coins, they set out for Keswick Station. After alighting, but before going to view the lakes, they decided to look at the black-lead pencil factory and to go down a lead mine. This was splendid fun. They slung a stout rope over one of the schoolroom beams and fastened an old waste-paper basket at one end, several boys holding the other. A small boy now volunteered to descend the mine in the cage. He got into the basket and held on tightly with both hands. Then the boys hauled him up

to the beam and afterwards slowly let him down again.
By this time some of the boys had converted themselves
into miners, all pretending to work diligently. The visitor
was shown over the mine — asking questions all the while
— and on leaving had a lead pencil given to him as a
souvenir. Leaving Keswick (which they always connected
in their minds with lead pencils, the mine, and the waste-
paper basket!), they again took train to Windermere.
Here they had rigged up a grand hotel with the magic
sign "Teas provided" outside. I wondered what this had
to do with geography, but later I found out their ingenuity.
The travelers admired the lake, hired a boat and were
rowed about in it, talked to the boatman and to some
fishermen whom they passed, talked and listened to the
lake fairies (one of whose speeches is recorded above), and
finally went to the hotel. Here they decided to sleep for
the night and, sending for the proprietress, they asked if
they might have fresh fish for supper.

LANDLADY. Oh, yes! I will send my man to catch
some for you.

TRAVELER. Does he catch them in the lake?

LANDLADY. No, in the river which runs from the lake.

TRAVELER. What river is that?

LANDLADY. The Leven.

TRAVELER. Which will be the next nearest lake for us
to visit?

LANDLADY. I should say Coniston Water, and there
you may see Ruskin's house.

TRAVELER. Well, if that neighborhood has scenery as grand as this, Ruskin knew where he could study the beauties of nature.

LANDLADY. Oh, the lakes are not only beautiful, they are useful, also. There is one called Thirlmere, a very beautiful and clear lake. It supplies Manchester with drinking water.

TRAVELER. But Manchester must be at least seventy miles away!

LANDLADY. I'm not good at figures, but I know the water is carried to Manchester in pipes.

TRAVELER. [*Takes out map and, after finding Thirlmere, moves his finger aside*] I see that Derwent Water is quite near Thirlmere, and here is Skiddaw marked to the north of it.

LANDLADY. Some people think Derwent Water the prettiest lake. At all events, the Derwent River is the only one of importance in this district. But Grasmere and Rydal Water are really the most interesting places to visit.

TRAVELER. And why is that?

LANDLADY. Because so many poets and authors have lived there and written about them. You have heard of Wordsworth? The last years of his life were passed at "Rydal Mount," a beautiful house, and he is buried in Grasmere churchyard.

TRAVELER'S LITTLE BOY. Yes, father. We have learned a good many of Wordsworth's poems and read a good many more. One is called "The Cumberland Beggar," and another is "The Pet Lamb." There are many about Duddon River too.

LANDLADY. There's hardly a rock or stream or nook about this part which he did not visit and write about. My grandfather often met him out on his long tramps over the hills and dales. Coleridge, a great friend of his, Southey, and De Quincey also lived in this neighborhood, and wrote about it.

LITTLE BOY. Oh, dad, I know something that Southey wrote. It was "The Falls of Lodore." Do take me to see the falls. They must be wonderful.

LITTLE GIRL. When the Spanish Armada came to England, the people lighted a beacon fire on Skiddaw. We read about it in a piece of poetry called "The Armada," by Macaulay.

TRAVELER. Well, we will go to bed now, and to-morrow morning the first thing, we will do what Wordsworth did: we will tramp over hill and dale, and see all we can.

LANDLADY. Ah! that's if it does n't rain, sir!

TRAVELER. Ha, ha! That's a sly hit at the climate. I know you are noted for having the rainiest climate in England. What causes it?

LANDLADY. Some say it is the moist winds from the Atlantic.

TRAVELER. I suppose the mountains attract the great rainfall and cause the great lakes at the same time.

LANDLADY. Well, we are not so badly off as the people at Seathwaite, near here. They say it rains there every day of the year but one!

TRAVELER. Well, now to bed, and let us all wish for a fine day to-morrow.

This would end the first scene, and the children would next proceed on their "tramp," pretending to visit the places discussed and making up little conversations with the people they found there. They bought picture post-cards of the "Lake District," and appointed a boy or girl to sell them at each place for cardboard coins. Some of their remarks were very apt. For instance, when they came to some supposed rough, rocky mountain paths, they pretended to find a primrose, and said: "That must be Wordsworth's 'Primrose of the Rock.'" Then they found a little nook (in the playground which was now their "Cumberland") with a violet growing in it. It was really a rockery which they had made years before for their first nature study. One said: "Oh! there's a beautiful water-fall. See how it sparkles and foams!" And another chimed in, "Look at those great bowlders 'fleeced with moss,' and those shady trees dipping into the water!" "Oh, I am sure," added a third, "this is the nook which Wordsworth wrote of, where 'the violet of five summers reappears and fades unseen by any human eye.'"

On another afternoon they arranged a most realistic visit to the Falls of Lodore, to take place in their play-time, and prepared for during their dinner hour. Some time before this they had dug a deep trench along one side of their playground in order to drain off the stagnant water which interfered with play and drill. At the lower end of the trench they had knocked a hole in the boundary wall and inserted a drainpipe, which, when the trench was full, caused a miniature waterfall into the field outside

Photograph by Clarke and Hyde

NORTH AMERICAN INDIANS AT MEALTIME. IN THE BACKGROUND ENGLISH

SETTLER PLOWING

the wall. The boys dug away the bank under the drain-pipe to emphasize this. But on the day of the great visit to the Falls of Lodore the weather was cloudless and there was every indication that we should have an empty trench. But there had to be a Falls of Lodore; so a council was held, and the boys overcame the difficulty. They carried out an old blackboard, placed it against the wall over the trench in a slanting position, and heaped great stones all over it — to hide the fact that it was a blackboard, and also to give an appearance of realism to the " splashing and dashing " mentioned in the poem. One boy filled a tin bathtub with water. At the appointed time, when the travelers, armed with the book containing Southey's poem, arrived at the spot, the boy (who had filled the bathtub and raised it to the top of the wall, where he sat astride holding it) slowly tipped it over, and behold ! the Falls of Lodore.

The same part of the playground was admirably suited to the purposes of the older pupils when playing " Switzer-land." They amplified the blackboard idea and carried out the top of a movable platform, which they placed slant-wise against the wall and styled a " glacier," and which they climbed with great difficulty and much display of alpenstock, ice ax, rope, and guides. Needless to say, the " guides " had to be well up in their subjects and know the names and peculiarities of all the "peaks" of the play-ground. The older pupils could construct really good and interesting plays and did not make the textbook source of their information quite so obvious. They had evidently learned the "art of concealing art." Not only did they rig up a glacier, but they named it and placed it correctly with reference to other physical features. They even had adventures on it. Falling over the edge was tumbling into a crevasse. One of their number fell over, and the guides and others performed a gallant rescue. The Swiss game was not complete without an avalanche, which came while the tourists (who were the life of the game) were sleeping in a hillside cottage. Some one who possessed a carved wooden model of a Swiss cottage brought it to school. After that the "cottage" was always the model on a projecting table under which the inmates sat. The Swiss girls (having practiced considerably by themselves) treated us to Swiss "jodeling." Herds of cows and goats were driven along, and the fact elicited from the peasants that the milk was to be condensed and sent to England — probably retailed in our own town. Samples of Swiss milk chocolate were taken (and evidently found up to par!) and questions asked as to the size, government, education, language, and history of Switzerland.

Of course the older girls could easily arrange "properties" for this game, and they were always giving us little surprises. On one occasion it was a nice little dairy that they had rigged up, with clean-scrubbed, red flowerpots for dairy pans. On another occasion it was the decoration of the Swiss cottage with gentians and "edelweiss" (make-believe, of course). The boys made up a St. Bernard game with two of their number as St. Bernard dogs with little tin pails strapped in front of them. It was noticeable that they always exhausted every available authority in these geography games, and, as they themselves used to say, " If we went over to those countries, we should not feel at all strange now ; we should know what to look for."

When we played " France " the girls provided a little surprise. Of course, being quite a rural school in an agricultural district, French was not a subject in our curriculum. But the girls had been much interested in the little lessons in French given in the " Children's Encyclopedia," and they surprised us with a few little phrases such as : *oui, madame; au revoir; bon jour*, and others relating to the voyage, the weather, etc., all of which I welcomed as stimulating ambition and a step on the right road.

Canada was found to be particularly well adapted to form the subject of a play of this kind, and several games were made up by the older pupils on the different parts of the Dominion. The important feature was that the pupils avoided monotony by not treating any two districts quite alike.

In their first Canadian game they dealt with the "lumbering" district, some of them impersonating animals, settlers, and Indians. The latter wore striped blankets, rugs, or tablecloths to distinguish them from settlers and had fearful and wonderful headdresses made of feathers sewed on wide tape. Sometimes they even took the trouble to paint their faces. We possessed one pair of real Indian shoes decorated with the peculiar colored grasswork of the North American Indian, which were worn by the most important " chief." The Indians would hunt the beaver, sometimes shooting but more often trapping them. They were made to go on the "warpath," uttering strange whoops and shrieks and waving tomahawks and scalping knives (cut from stiff cardboard). They would then make their exit, and the lumbermen would enter. A small tree would be brought into school and fixed upright in a tub. Then the lumbermen would appear and mark out trees to be cut. The trees would be chopped down, and, in conversation, the men would let us know that the trees were being cut, but could not be floated down the river until the "freshets" started. These, they explained, were sudden risings of the rivers which occurred very quickly in the springtime, owing to the sudden thawing of the snow and ice. The ice was supposed to break up, and the men would pretend to push the logs into the water. This was great fun, for one boy brought some long pieces of chains, and we pretended to throw the logs into the stream and form rafts. Then the boys gave us a realistic bit of acting, jumping on the rafts and guiding them along by pushing the river bank (floor !) with poles. They really did manage to slide their logs along, much to the joy of the enthusiastic onlookers. Then amid tense excitement they made their logs jam, and the men pretended to break the ice. Some of their number were "injured" at this point and had to receive "first aid" from their companions. They would bring out in their dialogue the names of the rivers, as they floated down them, and of the ports to which they would presently come. The logs would be sawed into "deals" and shipped, the boys who were lumbermen quickly becoming men

NORTH AMERICAN INDIANS KILLING ANIMALS

working the steam saws at Ottawa. While the men were chopping down the trees, in the "winter" scene, traders would come and bargain for the wood. The talk would take place in the "shanty," rigged up with easels, blackboards, and benches. Then other boys dressed as Indians would steal in and listen outside the shanty. They would offer skins to the lumbermen and exchange them for corn, tobacco, beads, and whisky. Some of the rougher lumbermen would pretend to lie in wait for a trader to rob and kill him; after a scuffle he would escape on his rough horse. While this was going on the Indians would loot the shanty and steal away.

What always struck me most forcibly was the fact that nothing — the amount of preparation, the arrangement of multitudinous details, the memorizing of long parts, the making of copious notes — ever seemed to be looked upon as the least trouble. The truth was that all these things constituted healthy brain and bodily activity for normal children and developed them equally in all directions. It seems to me that it is only when the balance of nature is upset that boredom, fag, and "it's-too-much-trouble-itis" sets in. And even adults never confess to weariness when they *want* to do anything : pleasure outbalances the other sensations.

When Australia was to be the subject of the play, the form was again slightly altered. This time it was the story of an emigrant. The emigrant's father and mother, an aged couple, were discovered sitting by the fire with their two sons. From their conversation it was made clear that the elder son was off to Australia on the morrow. The aged father said: "So you're off, my lad, to-morrow, thirteen thousand miles — 't is a long way to sail! And do ye tell me, lad, that you'll be right round t' other side of the world, with your feet pointing toward ours? However will ye keep from falling off?"

The mother chimed in here with: "Oh, dear! Oh, dear! To think I brought ye up for this — to go walking around on your head!" The two sons then explained everything as well as they could — about the world being round and revolving on its axis, and why people neither stand on their heads nor fly off into space. The second scene showed the elder son leaving Southampton, while his parents and brother waved him a tearful farewell. The chorus described Southampton and also the journey, as the "ship" slowly proceeded down the room. Maps were produced here — on the children's own initiative — and the places stopped at, as well as the port where the emigrant was to land, were correctly named and described. Arriving in the new country, the settler pretended to hunt for work. He got addresses of farmers who wanted hands from a boy who represented an agent. Calling on the first farmer, he asked for work.

FARMER. Where do you come from?

EMIGRANT. Oh, from Sussex.

FARMER. Ah! you are just the lad for me. Do you know anything about sheep?

EMIGRANT. Why, yes! The South Downs are noted for them.

FARMER. Then perhaps you can shoot a rabbit or two! I wish you 'd help me to get rid of a few. I am fairly overrun with them.

EMIGRANT. Ah! many's the young wild rabbit I've brought back for supper at home in Sussex.

In conversation like this the "farmer" engaged the "emigrant," and the conditions, climate, flora, fauna, etc., of the district were pointed out to him.

Another scene showed the emigrant, after several years had elapsed, with a sheep farm of his own. His "brother" from Sussex arrives on the scene, having come out to assist him. On his first day the emigrant and his brother take a ride round part of the farm (splendid opportunity to ride on another boy's back!), and we learn a little more, for as they ride they converse.

VISITOR. Why, you seem to have no grass here.

EMIGRANT. Ah, we are having a long, dry season, and it has been long enough to make every blade of grass dry up and wither away.

VISITOR. Then how do you feed your hundreds of sheep?

EMIGRANT. Oh, they eat those scrubby-looking desert shrubs that even the drought cannot kill. It is astonishing how nature provides those plants with the means to resist the dry weather and burning heat.

VISITOR. You appear to be glad of rain and do not call rainy weather "bad weather" as we often do in England.

EMIGRANT. Ah! you should see it when it *does* rain. Torrents — bucketsful! Rivers overflowing — floods everywhere — sheep drowned! It is a treat to stand out and soak in it.

VISITOR. Those are fine trees. What are they?

EMIGRANT. Eucalyptus, or gum trees. Some of those are two hundred fifty feet high and as much as twenty feet round the trunk. Those pretty trees near the house are acacias, or wattles. The eucalyptus trees look strange to you because their leaves are vertical instead of parallel to the ground, and they shed their bark instead of their leaves.

VISITOR. I know why their leaves are twisted so. It is to present the smallest surface to the scorching sun, otherwise the leaves would be burnt up and the tree would die. There are dwarf beans which grow in our gardens at home in Sussex that turn their leaves so during the hottest part of the day for the same reason.

EMIGRANT. I fancy there's another reason. Leaves so turned allow every drop of rain to fall close to the tree and keep none from the ground. Besides, the leaves in that position offer no lodging place for dust, which clogs the pores of leaves, and we sometimes have dreadful sand-laden winds, brickdust winds they are called.

VISITOR. You have some queer animals about; whatever is that creature?

EMIGRANT. Oh, our native animals are queer, and, like the native plants, of no use to man. That's a kangaroo with a young kangaroo in its pouch. I'll show you a platypus — an animal which has feet and bill like a duck and which lays eggs. We have beautiful birds — one is the lyre bird — but you will not hear the song birds of old England. What would n't I give to hear a missel thrush sing again!

VISITOR. Well, at any rate, I see one familiar friend here!

EMIGRANT. Who's that?

VISITOR. The Scotch thistle.

EMIGRANT. Yes, however it got here, it means to stay. The government is spending pots of money in trying to get rid of it. Probably it came over with the Scotch cattle and won't go until they do!

VISITOR. There go more rabbits! Upon my word the whole place is alive with them.

EMIGRANT. Yes, in ten years they did $15,000,000 worth of damage in Victoria, and the sparrows are nearly as bad. But we send millions of rabbit skins to England to be used in making felt hats and furs.

VISITOR. When I came to the railway terminus on my way to Southampton to join the ship, I saw a lot of frozen sheep sewed up in white cloths ready to be put in the train for London. The cloths were stamped with the name "Barnes & Downey."

EMIGRANT. Well, I never! That's the name of the firm to which I send my sheep. They are both Sussex men, and it so happens that I expect them to-day. There's a trap driving up to the gate of our farmhouse now. You will soon meet an Englishman.

[*They trot back to the end of the room, called the farm-house.* BARNES *and* DOWNEY *drive in, seated in a soapbox "buggy." They shake hands with the* Emigrant *and his* Brother]

VISITOR. Why, I remember you! Are n't you old Teddie Barnes, who went to school with me, and used to help us act our lessons so well?

BARNES. Oh, yes! But you must n't call me that now, you know, for I 've grown to be a man.

VISITOR. [*Laughing*] Ah, well, I 'd like to make closer acquaintance with you!

DOWNEY. Well, what have we for dinner to-day — sheep, mutton, ram, or lamb?

EMIGRANT. [*To* younger Brother] That 's an old joke of ours, but it is pretty nearly true!

VISITOR. Well, in old England it seems to be mutton and beef, beef and mutton.

Then, in course of conversation, it is shown that the "emigrant," who is now called a "squatter," owns ten thousand sheep, and as the pasturage is scantier than in England, this means many thousands of acres of land. The "shepherds" are mounted men who spend all day in the saddle. The "agents" tell of the hundreds of frozen sheep and bales of wool which pass through their hands yearly. So the game ends for the day, to be varied on another occasion by taking the divisions of Australia separately and showing, among other things, the famous "Broken Hill" silver mine.

Just as the children were interested in playing their "Australia" games a friend visited the school, fresh from a tour in New Zealand. Such an attentive audience surely never listened to geographical lecturer before! Those eager children had quickly grasped the fact that there was "copy"—otherwise games—to be secured, and no sooner was the visitor's back turned than they were busy concocting a "New Zealand" game. They planned out three scenes, namely:

1. New Zealand and visit of Captain Cook; murder of Captain Cook; cannibals eating human flesh; introduction of pigs; natives converted from cannibalistic tastes, owing to superior flavor (!) of pigs.

2. Early settlers civilizing the natives.

3. Present-day conditions; sheep farms; description of flora and fauna; frozen-meat exports; native customs as shown by funeral ceremony of Maoris, including Maori "crying lady" (who shed tears from a small bottle of water hidden in a large handkerchief).

This game included some fine realistic effects, for one boy brought a tame jackdaw which did duty for the quaint native wingless bird, the apteryx. As a grand finale the boys constructed a model volcano, which "worked" satisfactorily with the aid of a heap of sand and some fireworks.

New Zealand would not have been complete without some references to hot springs and mud lakes. The way the boys introduced them was funny. They supposed themselves to be travelers mounted on ponies, and rode up and down the room, pointing out the scenery in this fashion : "What a splendid bit of scenery! What is that snow-covered mountain?" "Oh, that is Mount Cook, named after Captain Cook, who —— Oh — h — h!" Here the "pony" reared suddenly, almost throwing the boy off its back, and refused to go forward. Its rider tried to force it on. The other riders dismounted and ran toward him. One of their number fell prone on the floor and appeared to struggle, as though in the water. "Help, help, drag me out!" he yelled. "What is it?" they all cried, as they pulled him out. "A mud lake, I expect," answered the victim. "What was it like?" they all asked. "Hot," replied the muddy one; "*I* should have been *cooked* if I had stayed in there long." The whole game, in fact, teemed with incidents extremely funny to an adult spectator (although perfectly serious so far as the pupils were concerned). For instance, when "Captain Cook" was overwhelmed by the "cannibals" and just about to die, he called out to his men : "Escape for your lives, men! You can do me no good. Farewell! Tell them in England that I died a *noble man!*" As if Captain Cook would have found time to brag, or that there could be anything noble in being ignominiously eaten by degraded cannibals! Not that this was in itself funny; it was the melodramatic strut and pose of the juvenile "Cook" which almost convulsed one.

The "savages" were made to speak a kind of broken English, interspersed with squeaks and "wows." They devoured "human" arms made of brown paper, stuffed. When persuaded to abstain from such delicacies, in favor of stuffed brown-paper pig, they had an eye to the main chance, for they said: "No let us eatee mans any more. We catchee mans and eatee them. But p'r'aps some day mans catchee us and eatee *us*. Not safe. Better all eatee pig!"

Very comical, too, was the boys' attempt to show how natives were civilized. They pretended to chop down trees for wood with which to build houses. The "natives" gathered round and watched them from a distance. Soon the "settlers" beckoned to the natives and held out colored cloth and strings of beads, etc. The natives pressed forward, saying, "Me? Me?" and holding out their hands. The settlers handed them the axes and pointed to the trees, making signs to them to "chop-chop," and then pointing to the beads, etc. But the savages, taking the axes, turned to attack the settlers, who, after a struggle, drove them back and once more showed them what they wanted them to do before they could have the beads. At last they made them do the work and duly rewarded them. Observe that the childish idea of civilizing was by means of teaching handicraft, or, shall we say, of utilizing handicraft to the advantage of the more civilized.

The funeral ceremony of the native Maoris had been described at length by our visitor, but much had been left to the imagination, as, for instance, the spoken words. The boys enacting the scene blacked their faces — shall I confess it? — by rubbing their hands up the chimney.

They laid the dead "chief" on a bench and then ceremoniously brought mats instead of wreaths, — again I hesitate, but truth will out, — the school doormats, which they placed over the chief! (I must remark that the mats were well shaken.) They laid the "spear" of the dead chief beside him. The head of this spear was a hollow beef bone, to remind us that there is a lack of minerals in New Zealand, and that the cannibals utilized human bones instead. The children also brought to school other small bones, which they pretended were native needles, fishhooks, and other things formed from human bones. From the "Children's Encyclopædia" they found how to cut out boomerangs. Imagine their joy on discovering a real boomerang in our Free Museum!

The part which taxed their ingenuity considerably was reached when the chiefs attending the funeral had to speak. The "crying lady" (albeit a boy!) could perform *her* part to a nicety, so she was told to howl loudly whenever the chieftains failed for lack of words. What they did say, I remember, was something like this:

FIRST CHIEF. Oh, he was brave and he was noble!
SECOND CHIEF. He had the heart of a lion.
THIRD CHIEF. And the legs of a fox!
FOURTH CHIEF. He had the appetite of an ostrich.
FIRST CHIEF. He slew many enemies.
SECOND CHIEF. Yea, he slew his thousands!
THIRD CHIEF. He could throw the boomerang.
FOURTH CHIEF. He could climb the gum trees.

All this was punctuated by solemn marches to and fro, while spears were rattled on the ground at intervals, and the " crying lady " howled in the pauses.

Then the chiefs had a feast cooked in the native way, as described to them by the visitor.

When we had finished our " New Zealand " games I realized that, personally, I knew far more of that place than I had ever known before. Of course names of places had been duly noted, as well as manners, customs, and history. And while mentioning history, it may interest my readers to know that our " Captain Cook " managed to introduce, in an ingenious way, the history of the places he explored. In calling at Tasmania he said : " Oh, this island was discovered by the Dutch. I remember that Tasman called here. He named it Van Diemen's Land." And when he " sighted " the next land, he said : " This must be the land discovered by those clever Dutchmen again. They called it New Zealand, after their home." All this was brought out in a conversational way by the " Captain " and his " First Mate."

Occasionally, to be quite sure that all they said was understood, the " producers " of the play would call upon the chorus to " come out and see if you can go through our parts."

Could they ? It was just a case of rushing for the chief parts, regardless of the difficulties. Of course this only spurred the older pupils on to make their parts fuller and more nearly perfect, and in this way a healthy rivalry was promoted between the different classes.

Frequently, too, the older pupils would write out in their recreation time little geography plays, abridged and adapted from their own plays, for the lower-class pupils. I would allow them to conduct these,—quite by themselves, —and so a new school "tone" or tradition was formed. I would often hear the younger pupils saying, "When I get up in the 'big room' I am going to be Captain Cook, and you can be a cannibal," and such things.

In my opinion, the best result of this method of studying geography was the way in which the pupils — left to themselves — connected geography and history details with real persons and real deeds. When they studied Africa, they played games about Livingstone and other explorers, and in this way gradually unfolded the history and geography of Africa.

CHAPTER IX

ARITHMETIC AND COMPOSITION

ARITHMETIC may become a delightful subject when taught largely by means of plays. We first made our arithmetic games correlate with the week's nature study, taking care that they did not become haphazard and purposeless. For instance, it is quite possible, when the weekly nature lesson happens to be on "acorns and oak trees" and the arithmetic lesson deals with the "six times table," to blend the two into a game rather than to play some purposeless game with acorns alone. The teacher may be quite methodical — as it behooves one to be in a subject like arithmetic — and yet, with the art of concealing art, she may prevent her method from obtruding itself upon the pupils' mental vision.

In a subject like arithmetic it is necessary that the teacher should "lead" a little more than in other subjects. From its very nature it is evident that the children cannot be allowed a perfectly free hand, or chaos would result. But after a good beginning has been made, they may quite safely be allowed to help and suggest in the preparation of plays almost as much as in such subjects as geography and history. Here is an example of a simple game which Grade I children helped to "make up":

Six boys pretended to be oak trees. They filled their pockets and hands with acorns. They pretended that their outstretched arms were branches. Another boy represented the north wind, and ran round puffing and shaking the "trees." Down fell the acorns! Harry pretended to be a little boy with a basket gathering acorns. Two other boys were pigs and ate up the acorns which were left. They merely pretended to eat, and in reality pocketed them.

"How many have you eaten?" asked the teacher.

The class wrote down the answers of both boys.

"How many have you, Harry?"

Harry duly counted and his answer was jotted down.

"Now, how many are left on the trees?"

This was noted, too.

"Then, if Harry gathered so many, and the pigs ate a total of so many, and so many were left on the trees, how many acorns were there at first? How many fell from the tree?" etc.

Then all the class worked out the answers and wrote down the sums in the correct form.

Tables can easily be learned when "played" with bunches of snowdrops or other flowers. A little girl selling snowdrops at so much a bunch with so many in each bunch — say six (the children having made up one bunch each) — may teach her companions the "six times table" unconsciously.

GIRL. Buy my snowdrops to-day, lady? Only one cent a bunch!

LADY. How many are there in a bunch?

GIRL. Six, lady.

LADY. Then I will have two bunches and that will make twelve snowdrops.

Enter Mother *with three little* Children

GIRL. Snowdrops, lady? Only one cent for a bunch of six!

MOTHER. Oh, how pretty they look! Yes, I will buy a little nosegay for each of my three children. How many snowdrops shall we have altogether then?

CHILDREN. Three sixes — that will be eighteen.

MOTHER. And if I have a bunch, too?

CHILDREN. *Four* sixes! Why, that will be twenty-four.

[GIRL *goes to greengrocer's shop kept by small* Boy]

GIRL. Can you take some of my snowdrops to-day, sir? You can have them at five bunches for four cents — six in a bunch.

BOY. Yes, I'll have four cents' worth. Looks a small lot for thirty snowdrops, does n't it?

GIRL. You can count them, sir. [*Waits*] All correct?

BOY. If I had *six* bunches, it would n't look much more, and yet there would be — let's see — thirty-six flowers.

And so on, varying the conversations until the table is complete. The same game may supply a good mental arithmetic lesson in dealing with short money sums.

We all know how, as children, we delighted in playing with dough or putty. Acting on this knowledge, I always taught the earliest lessons of arithmetic with the aid of some flour and water dough. With this children can play at making little loaves. It is not difficult for a child to master the fact that "ten units equal one ten," when he has made ten little dough loaves out of a piece of dough the same size as one big loaf. He soon learns addition and subtraction if he collects all the "little loaves" and makes one big loaf out of every ten small ones, for he sees the "answer" before him in the concrete.

The next game naturally suggests itself, namely, playing store. Our first store was a dry-goods shop, and I left the girls to prepare the details. They threw a great deal of enthusiasm and energy into their work and prepared a game which interested all of us for several lessons. They made cabinets and chests of drawers with the aid of cardboard boxes, using brass buttons for handles and making the drawers so that they could be pulled in and out. Fathers and brothers became interested and sent worn-out silk ties and frayed collars for the "Gentlemen's Department." Mothers sent treasures in the shape of any small garments, now out of use — all washed clean — for the "Ready-made Department." One of the older girls achieved a triumph, for she spent several evenings plaiting raffia or mat (such as is used in tying up lettuce) in a good imitation of straw plait. The "plaits," when sewed together, made splendid French creations in dolls' hats, especially when plumed with chickens' feathers. Later she became more ambitious and made hats large enough for children to wear. These the "mothers," who were prospective purchasers, tried on their "children's" heads and bargained for. The saleswomen displayed the charms of the hats, and the cashier at the desk took the money and gave change — using cardboard coins, of course. A feature of this game was the set of real billheads, such as are used by real stores, which were supplied me by a well-known firm for advertisement.

From some source or other the children procured the long strips of white and colored paper which paper hangers cut off wall paper, called trimmings. These they made up into neat rolls and styled ribbons or tapes. One girl carefully cut out white paper "embroidery" by folding the strips several times and then cutting nicks and curves which, when the paper was unfolded, showed an imitation of a lace pattern. Others begged from the dry-goods stores the ribbon rolls with white paper interlinings (the paper which is rolled up with the ribbons on the roll) of various widths. The clerks in the stores, sympathizing with the object for which the rolls were intended, kindly saved both paper and rolls for the children, who colored these "ribbons" by means of crayon and paint. The object of all this trouble, they explained to me, was to enable them to ask for various colors and lengths, and be served properly without too much make-believe. When real ribbon was used, it could not be cut and then used again. With paper an exact length could be measured, cut, and taken away. A yard measure was fixed on the counter (desk) by means of drawing pins, and by its aid the children mastered the difficulties of yards, halves, quarters, and eighths. They received practice in calculating the prices of different lengths at so much per yard, in making out the bills correctly, and in giving the correct " change."

To add the necessary touch of realism the girls borrowed the school screen (an old four-fold one), so that they could have a proper door to open and shut. From the top corner of this door they hung a hand bell on string, so that each " customer's " arrival was duly announced by the tinkling of the bell, and everything was quite proper and " shoppy." I hardly need say that, since all this took place immediately in front of the class, there was no need for the teacher to *tell* the children to " pay attention," nor did she need to have any fears that the class was not thoroughly keen about adding up the various sums when they paid for their " goods." The pupils would not have been real children if they had not been desperately anxious to catch the cashier giving the wrong change.

A miniature post office, with tiny note paper and envelopes, stamps, telegram forms, and postal orders, gave rise to another game, which combined the writing of letters (composition), directing of envelopes, a little geography in the correct placing of the various towns, and arithmetic.

Land measuring with a real chain made a good game for the older boys, who by this means actually measured off and made a wheat field (to scale) in the playground. After watching it grow they had a real harvest (one boy brought his tame rabbit and hid it in the cornfield, so that, when the corn was cut, a real rabbit might be found !) and got a neighboring farmer to have their wheat threshed with his. The grain which he sent back they measured and then reckoned by proportion the amount which might have come from an ordinary-sized wheat field — prices, profits, etc. Further, they sent the bag of grain to the miller's to be ground, and the girls baked a loaf of bread out of the resulting flour. Could boyish enterprise do more? And, remember, the wheat field was planted on what had previously been hard, flinty playground — beaten down by generations of little children with sturdy legs and good strong boots! The young pioneers removed about two tons of flint and marl, with which they repaired the lane leading to the school, and filled the space with road drift and leaf mold of their own collecting. Thus the wheat field was quite a serious game, such as bigger boys would find to their taste.

Liquid measure was attacked by means of a milk shop, with (do not laugh!) chalky water for milk. Sea sand, when dry, answered admirably for sugar, and when wet might be cut out for butter, etc. So pounds, ounces, and drams soon presented few difficulties.

This short account by no means disposes of the arithmetic games, but it outlines a few of the most typical ones. We found out that very few children were naturally accurate when using weights and scales, but not a few corrected themselves of carelessness and clumsiness by these means, so that we were learning something besides arithmetic.

On "shopping" mornings the pupils would arrive much earlier than usual, shortly after 8 A.M., and on my arrival

I would find the "store" set out finely, looking quite like a real shop, with lines hung with goods on display, every window ledge spread with goods, and the proprietor or proprietress — positively bursting with importance — ticketing goods and generally taking stock.

The older girls invented a game to improve composition and teach letter writing. Its plot was briefly this : A merchant, seated in his office, soliloquizes on his need of an office boy. He decides to advertise in a local paper, and, taking up his pen, writes an advertisement enumerating the qualities he expects to find in the boy. He talks all the while he is writing, so that the class "hears" his letter being written, and all jot it down as he speaks. (This kept all the class employed, and really was an exercise in dictation as well.) After sealing, addressing, and stamping the envelope, he dropped it into our tiny post office. Another boy, who was postman, collected it and delivered it to the office of the newspaper. There the editor read it aloud, and, in dumb show, the advertisement was printed, the newspapers were given out to several small newsboys (who ran about crying, " Paper ! Paper-r-r ! "), and were duly bought by different boys supposed to be looking for situations. Three of these decide to apply for the position, and we follow the writing and composition of their letters, as was done with the merchant's letter. The boys were left quite to themselves to compose, and those who were waiting to write, went outside the door, so as not to hear the letters of the others. All these letters were posted and delivered, and the merchant read them aloud in his office.

He selected the best and wrote letters appointing an inter-view. The boys came and were questioned, etc. Finally, he engaged the one who wrote the best letter — as regards spelling, composition, and writing. The class used to help him in his choice from the letters they had jotted down. When the game was finished the teacher would turn the blackboard, on the back of which she had also written the letters, and, in a short talk, would point out defects or mistakes. The object of making the class, as well as the actors, write all the letters was that they might be better prepared, when their turn to be clerks came, to write an intelligible letter without wasting time.

CHAPTER X

NATURE STUDY NEWLY APPROACHED

EVEN nature study, which we had long made full use of in the form of direct study of nature, was newly approached by the children when they took matters in hand. They first made up a form of game which would supply the place of a nature ramble on the mornings when the weather was unfavorable for a real ramble.

One of the boys would impersonate the schoolmaster. A few of the other children would pretend to be flowers then in season and stand at intervals down the room, holding in their hands some specimens of the flower they impersonated. The rest of the class were the " class (of pupils) out for a ramble." They formed in twos and, setting out from one end of the room, arrived at the first " flower." On one occasion this happened to be a sweet-pea. The following dialogue then took place :

PUPIL. Oh, here is a pretty sweet pea hanging over this garden fence !

SWEET PEA. He is wrong. I am not *hanging* over it at all ! I climbed up here on purpose to look over at the sun. If he tries to pull me down he will find I am holding on quite firmly.

A NATURE-STUDY GAME—"QUESTIONING THE FLOWERS"

SECOND PUPIL. Good morning, pretty flower! We want to know more about you. Can you tell us anything?

SCHOOLMASTER. Look well and carefully at the flower and it will tell you its secrets.

SWEET PEA. [*In a high-pitched, weak voice*] I belong to a very large family. There are over four thousand seven hundred of us!

CHILDREN. [*In chorus*] Just fancy!

SWEET PEA. My family were always rather helpless, for they never grew a strong, upright stem among them. Years ago Queen Flora took pity on them and sent her court physician to examine their poor weak backs. He invented a way to hold their heads up by fitting them out with some little ropes to twine round a firm support—just as poor cripples have crutches. Now they are able to hold themselves up and climb much higher than most garden flowers.

THIRD PUPIL. I know one reason why you want to climb so high.

SWEET PEA. You may guess, and I will tell you if you are right.

THIRD PUPIL. You want to shoot your seeds as far away as possible in all directions. I remember you twist your pods in two spirals, giving a little jerk and twist at each turn, and so shoot your seeds out. If you are higher up, the seeds, of course, shoot farther.

SWEET PEA. Very good guess, little boy! I believe you are right. But now, little visitors, look at my tendrils. Can you guess what they are and where they came from?

FOURTH PUPIL. I think I can guess. They grow where leaves ought to be, and they look like "leaf bones" without the "flesh." Were they once leaves?

SWEET PEA. Clever boy! Yes, they are the remains of leaves. But instead of doing the work of leaves, they now work at clinging and holding on tightly.

FIFTH PUPIL. But you have a very funny stem. It is more like a leaf than a stem.

SWEET PEA. I wonder whether some little boy or girl can explain that. Think hard, and then try.

SIXTH PUPIL. I know. When the green "flesh" of some of your leaves stopped growing, there was then less leaf work being done; and you did not want *less* nourishment to help you climb, but more! So the material of which those leaves would have been made was used to make your stem wide and flat, so that it could do the work of a leaf.

SWEET PEA. Right again! You see, nature never wastes anything.

SCHOOLMASTER. Do you ever have any exciting times here in the garden?

SWEET PEA. Just at present there is the Sweet Pea and Blue Cornflower race on.

PUPILS. Oh, tell us about that!

SWEET PEA. Well, the White Sweet Pea and the Blue Cornflower wanted to find out which could grow the taller. The Blue Cornflower took great pains to strengthen her stems, for she knew how the strong winds blow even in June. The Sweet Pea waited for the Cornflower to grow,

A FAIRY PLAY — NATURE STUDY IDEALIZED

inch by inch; and then, artfully throwing out a tendril, she wound it securely round the Cornflower and drew herself up level with her rival. Look! You can see for yourselves, White Sweet Pea has thrown all kind feeling to the winds and has reared her head quite a foot above the Cornflower, and has cruelly twined her tendrils round even the Cornflower's blossoms, forcing them to support her.

SCHOOLMASTER. I have known some children like that. They will let others work and learn for them, and, instead of using their own brains and powers, they borrow from others.

The class would then pass on to the next flower, and another dialogue would take place. These plays were always the children's own. Generally the dialogue was impromptu, and went on in a kind of debate, during which many interesting things were discovered. For instance, in the early springtime one of the children impersonated the hazel catkin, and to illustrate the way in which the catkin is first stiff and almost upright, but afterwards limp and pendent, she held a string of beads pressed up so tightly on the string that they could be held in an upright position. Then she relaxed the string and showed how it immediately hung downward.

In the short specimen play which I have quoted, the "schoolmaster," in conjunction with the "flowers," had prepared his matter beforehand. But, none the less, the play was their own.

In connection with their nature study, and as a variant of the "Ramble" play, the girls used to make very pretty

"Fairy" plays, introducing stories on nature, which had been compiled from their nature study for the week. Generally these were written in verse, each fairy talking in couplets composed by herself. Into these plays they would weave the Morris dance, and generally they would borrow the folk music for their couplets.

One such game was called "Spring." A girl represented Queen Flora asleep in an empty garden. Suddenly a bright little girl, dressed to represent Sunshine, sprang in, touched the sleeping Queen Flora with her wand, and said: "Awake! I am the Fairy of Springtime, and I come to bid you awake!'

The queen slowly got up, and, seating herself on a throne (chair with curtains draped over it), said: "Call Fairy Aconite." Crinkled paper had been freely used in getting up costumes for the little crowd of "spring flowers" — correctly called by the queen in the order in which the spring flowers are expected to arrive. Each "fairy" had prepared a verse descriptive of her own personality and peculiarities, which she either said or warbled. When all were assembled, a dialogue ensued, summing up all they knew of spring and spring flowers; any verses of good poetry from standard authors bearing on the subject were repeated, something original in the way of dances or tableaux was arranged, and the "fairies" tripped off.

CHAPTER XI

MANUAL WORK

MUCH stress is now being laid on manual occupations in school, and, as I have previously remarked in this book, I nearly always found that the children's games connected themselves naturally with some form of handwork. I deemed this sufficient for children of the elementary-school age — that they should be able to use their fingers and hands without awkwardness in making for themselves such things as could not be more economically bought. This also had the double advantage of tending neither to spoil any one trade nor to neglect unduly any other. I have described how the children built their own shed when they played being " Tig," and how they excavated flint and marl from their playground to form a garden. In this way they formed a large vegetable garden in which they grew wonderful marrows, beans, peas, potatoes, cabbages, etc. They also planted cuttings of fruit trees, begged from their fathers, and in time had a very good fruit garden, with gooseberries, raspberries, black currants, strawberries, a peach tree, and a young apple tree. When they needed a glass seed frame, they made a crude one out of a packing case. Later, to encourage them, we bought one out of the school funds. Our object was not exactly to teach children living in an enlightened country like England that they must make, by tedious amateur processes, everything they needed. To that, on principle, I objected. I merely wanted to see how they set about to make something which would answer their purpose supposing they had not the wherewithal to buy the correct article. In the same way they made a little wooden fence for their vegetable garden (subsequent to a nocturnal visit from a cow, who ate up all their young cabbages and trampled everything else!) out of some old desks. To do them justice, the posts of that fence were "well and truly" driven home, for they stand there to this day.

Besides all this, the boys gradually made little semi-circular plots for separate flower gardens all round the playground, and in time converted a strip of ground under a south wall into a very fine herbaceous border, with an extremely good collection of flowers for every season, including some especially fine hollyhocks of every color and description. Thus the children's nature study called forth the accompanying manual work of simple carpentry and gardening, although these subjects *were not taught*.

The girls had their own form of handwork. Naturally this consisted chiefly of some branch of needlework, crochet, or knitting. Occasionally it took the form of cookery. At Christmas time they made "Christmas puddings," which were boiled and partaken of by the whole school on the day of breaking up for the Christmas holidays.

At another time pancakes were made in school, and, after being fried (each girl taking part by being allowed to beat the batter and fry one cake), they were eaten with great gusto. Other informal cookery included cake making, everything except the actual baking being done in school (the baking had to take place in the kitchen of the teacher's dwelling house), bread making, simple puddings, a molasses tart, and other delightful things. All these "dainties" were needed for games and were made as part of the play. On one occasion the girls wanted something more elaborate to answer the purpose of a wedding cake. I therefore showed them how to ice a cake, letting them assist me. One of the girls who assisted profited by the lesson, for she went home and practiced it again. Less than a year afterwards she gained a prize for an iced cake in a competition open to the county. A few years later she made and iced her own wedding cake. I tasted it and can testify that it left nothing to be desired — but another helping.

In their needlework the girls did a good deal of doll dressing, and the garments thus made were always cut out correctly to scale, being quite practical affairs in miniature. I never limited them as regards the "fancy" stitches, if they liked to use them. The trimmings were knitted by the children themselves, which led them to appreciate daintiness and neatness, and promoted a desire to make garments and lace for themselves as well as for the dolls. I am now convinced that children learn to dislike needlework only when it is presented to them in the form of large, unwieldy garments of ugly appearance, with long, tiring, monotonous seams. With miniature garments they get variety, and more quickly see a finished result of their labors. We permitted the use of the sewing machine for certain work in school — notably the long, tedious seams. The girls frequently dressed a doll, making for it a complete outfit suitable for a young working girl, even to outdoor garments and fashionable hats, and doing all the work, except the buttonholes, on the sewing machine. If I allowed them a free hand, it was delightful to find how many dainty little knickknacks they would make — tiny pocket handkerchiefs beautifully hemstitched, with the dolls' initials worked in the corner.

Sometimes we would play at dressmakers' shops, and little girls would come to be measured. Patterns of garments to measure would then be drafted and fitted, amid the criticism and advice of the onlookers. This gave rise to investigations into prices and quantities of material; and, naturally, the questioning came, not from the teacher, but from the children who were playing "dressmakers."

Of course we had included in our library some good books on pattern making and cutting, so that the girls soon found out how to get a good pattern and preserved all their successful ones for future use.

CHAPTER XII

AFTER SCHOOL AGE

THUS far I have dealt with the dramatic method as used in the elementary school for pupils under fourteen years of age. In this short chapter I should very much like to outline briefly the way in which the work, begun in the schoolroom, entered the home and after-school life.

Just as the nature-study movement filtered through the children's conversations at home until the parents imbibed it and went for nature rambles on Sunday afternoons with their children, so the dramatic method soon took hold on the home life.

It was not many years before older pupils, remembering the interesting plays in which they had joined at school, and wishing to do more than help their younger brothers and sisters to make properties, came and asked me to assist them during their winter evenings to act some suitable plays. The result of this was that we organized a sort of dramatic club for men, and after one or two false starts in the choice of plays, we hit upon a Shakespearean play suitable to be played by men. We first essayed to act one scene from Shakespeare's " Julius Cæsar " — the murder scene. Our cast consisted entirely of workingmen of the village — some were fathers of pupils, others, themselves old pupils. It was quite an inspiration to observe how really interested they all were in learning their parts, in discussing them, in studying them so as to bring out all that Shakespeare intended. They would frequently have long discussions over the meanings of words and allusions in the play, and went so far as to buy histories of Rome to clear up doubtful points and to get their costumes and properties correct in detail.

When one scene was mastered, however, the men were enthusiastic and demanded more. So we added another scene, and so on, until the complete play, minus the scene introducing Portia and Calpurnia, was well known. Then we engaged a hall and gave the play to an enthusiastic, overflowing audience. But the actual performance of the play is not the point I wish to emphasize; it is the fact that the men were educated enough to find ample amusement in one of Shakespeare's least droll plays. So much were they really interested that on one wet Saturday they spent eight consecutive hours (with a short interval for tea) in rehearsing in their Roman costumes. At the outset we had intended to meet one evening in the week. Toward the end the men would hardly be content without five meetings a week.

Their properties, although mostly of their own making, were quite correct; and the scene in which Brutus and Cassius quarrel, and where Cæsar's ghost appears, was so artistically gotten up, and so well acted, that it called forth

MOTHERS' DRAMATIC FOLK SONGS

(One mother is disguised in her husband's smock and gaiters)

the admiration of old and hardened newspaper critics on big London dailies.

The matter did not end there, for the *mothers* of the village not only acted plays but invented them. They, too, met at the school—which thus became a real center of light and learning—and there practiced plays written by one of their number. The first of these was entitled "A Cup of Tea," and contained some good local hits. Another play was patriotic and written *in verse!* The mothers also practiced the Morris dance and dramatized folk songs just as the scholars in the day school were doing. In the latter art they excelled, for they had a good store of the Sussex folk songs.

Comical in the extreme was their "band" of various instruments, which they managed to play tunefully. Really it seemed as if we had reached the ideal state of village life, and had made one or two steps toward reintroducing "Merrie England." Whether this was a result of the school method I leave others to judge, but let no one be afraid that the result of such teaching will be to set the whole community "acting mad." I have heard of none of the everyday work of the village being neglected, but I did observe that there were a few more cheerful faces to be seen among those who took part in the work.

Certain it is that one result of this kind of education will be to foster the good taste of our people, developing the capacities of our children and enabling them to find their propensity in choosing their life's career.

It seems to me that children trained on the lines indicated very inadequately in this book will be well fitted to take their part in the world. They will at least have had a fuller childhood than some of their predecessors, and, having acted well their parts in school, we will send them forth confidently, remembering that "all the world's a stage."

INDEX